OUTLAW TALES
of South Dakota

OUTLAW TALES
of South Dakota

True Stories of the Mount Rushmore State's
Most Infamous Crooks, Culprits, and Cutthroats

T. D. Griffith

TWODOT®

GUILFORD, CONNECTICUT
HELENA, MONTANA
AN IMPRINT OF THE GLOBE PEQUOT PRESS

A · TWODOT® · BOOK

Map by M. A. Dubé © 2008 Morris Book Publishing, LLC

Library of Congress Cataloging-in-Publication Data is available on file.
ISBN 978-0-7627-4342-1

Manufactured in the United States of America
10 9 8 7 6 5 4 3 2

For Nyla, who knows there's a little outlaw in each of us.

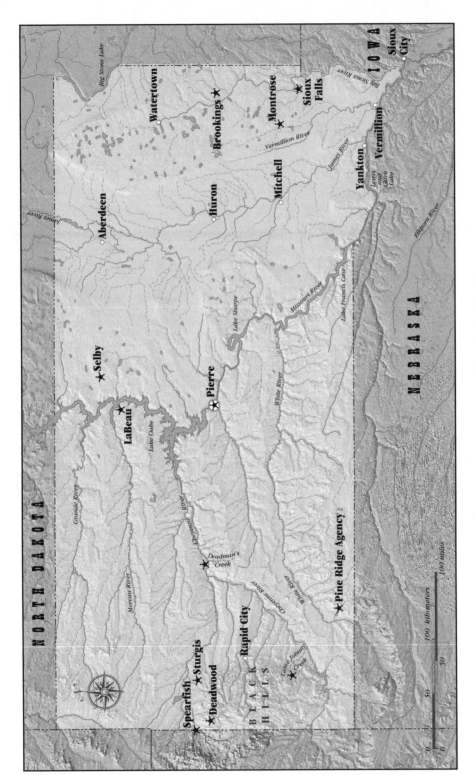

SOUTH DAKOTA

Contents

Acknowledgments

History is often defined by those who write it. In the case of *Outlaw Tales of South Dakota*, history's course has been charted by a variety of individuals and organizations that strive to preserve the stories of our treasured past, while embracing many of the legends that still give it the luster and patina of time. Kudos and my deepest appreciation are reserved for Carol A. Jennings, government archivist for the South Dakota State Historical Society, whose knowledge of South Dakota's collections and research expertise are reflected in virtually every page of this book. This tome of tales also could not have been realized without the expertise and guidance of Mary Kopco, director of Deadwood's Adams Museum & House, and her capable associates, Jerry Bryant, Arlette Hansen, Kate Bentham, and Darrel Nelson. So, too, did Deadwood Library director Jeanette Moodie assist with her gentle smile and welcome direction.

So many members of the Association of South Dakota Museums provided insights and knowledge of the characters and criminals who are inexorably linked to this state's past. It is with thanks that I acknowledge their contributions, particularly those of Linda Velder and the Newell Museum, Bill Hoskins at the Siouxland Heritage Museums, and countless others who were pestered for anecdotes and directions to the nearest tall tale often relegated to a musty storeroom or a brittle spindle of microfilm.

As with any project of this scope, I stumbled upon kindred souls who share a love of the past and endeavor to preserve it. Retired *Sioux Falls Argus Leader* reporter C. John Egan Jr. wasn't informed until his midlife that his grandfather had been erroneously executed for a crime he didn't commit. John's own book, *Drop Him Till He Dies*, provided incredible detail of the Egan case and I thank him for his personal insights. Appreciation also is extended to my old friend Larry Atkinson and the *Mobridge Tribune.*

Special thanks to my editor, Pat Straub, who shares a love of clear mountain streams and dry flies, as well as the lure and lore of the Old West. And finally, to my wife, Nyla, a fellow author who understands that research and writing are too often solitary pursuits, I pledge my undivided attention, at least until the next project too attractive to pass up.

Introduction

They hid in the shadows, these outlaws. Often desperate and sometimes brave, they preyed on those more fortunate and killed when so inclined, before making tracks for the hinterland.

In the latter part of the nineteenth century and half of the twentieth, a ragtag collection of cop killers, common crooks, muggers, and their molls made their way across the vast expanses of South Dakota's contribution to the Great Plains. Some did it on horseback, holding out in boxed canyons or dank caves. Others stole away slumped behind the damp steering wheel of a stolen car, ever watchful for lawmen who might be lurking behind the next tree or door or windshield.

It was relatively easy to conceal oneself in America's outback, and so South Dakota afforded ample protection. It was then, as it is now, one of the last best places to hide. Even today there are areas of South Dakota so sparsely populated that they are measured by square miles per person rather than people per square mile. In countless locations you can still see one hundred miles to the horizon and retrace one hundred years in a day. And so it goes with *Outlaw Tales of South Dakota*.

Outlaws in the early days of white settlement of Dakota Territory encountered few obstacles, excepting of course the well-armed man who objected to a perceived slight or who held that which the outlaw wanted. Marshals, of whom there were few, roamed whole territories hunting villains immortalized on well-worn wanted posters. Some of these lawmen were worse than the criminals they sought, but in so many instances they were infinitely better shots.

By and large, the law came late to western South Dakota. In fact, it was the last region on America's frontier to be mapped. The 1868 Fort Laramie Treaty had prevented white settlement of all the lands between the Missouri River and the Bighorn Mountains, at least until George

Armstrong Custer's 1874 Black Hills Expedition confirmed the presence of gold. Overnight the quiet canyons and gentle brooks became bastions for those seeking a better life, with hammers pounding and sluices running. Few struck it rich, although many were struck dead by disagreement and greed. The law was often settled by the quickest gun rather than the loosest tongue.

When the proprieties of law finally did arrive, first with territorial courts and then with statehood in 1889, not all of the newly minted South Dakotans recognized the benefits of the change. Still others of Native American extraction, humbled and miserable on reservations where they subsisted solely on government handouts, longed for the life they had known, an existence inexorably linked to the seasons, the land, and the buffalo herds on which they had once relied.

Later, when the Dust Bowl visited the plains and dried up every hope, leading to the greatest of economic depressions, the crooks, cutthroats, and connivers still sought every convenience, no matter its rightful owner. More often than not, their miserable lives ended at the wrong end of a loaded gun or the decades-long idleness of a lonely prison cell. One walked free, while another succumbed to electrocution wearing a $3 football helmet.

Although well tried and duly convicted, not all of the men that the territorial, state, and federal courts sent to their deaths were actually guilty, as the story of homesteader Thomas Egan explains. But that didn't really matter at the time. So many of the South Dakotans who greeted the arrival of decency, good judgment, and citified laws could not be inconvenienced with legal details or rights of appeal. Slow to advance from the immediacy of vigilante justice, in South Dakota's earliest days some death penalty cases were dispatched with greater speed than is a DUI today.

Lawbreakers and desperados were certainly as elusive then as they are now. By nature they didn't generally sit for portraits or favor inter-

Execution of Charles Brown *Photo courtesy of the Adams Museum*

views with the press. Retracing their footsteps and bullet holes some-times a century after the fact is not without its challenges, nor is it rife with definitive accounts or lacking in contradictions. It is with that stark reality that I approached this work, not seeking to commemorate the criminal, or mistakenly honor the condemned man with the heart of gold or the lawman who lent his life to evil pursuits. Discerning fact from fiction in any outlaw's tale is a lot like pushing rope, challenging yet futile. Pursuing a promising trail littered with microfilm and smudged newspaper accounts sometimes leads only to a dead end of pettifoggery and obfuscation. With studious research a grand tale of bravery and daring sometimes only lends itself to recounting as a sad tale of butch-ery and a final fate at the gallows. When the legends are tossed aside, sometimes all that lingers is an unpalatable truth.

These, then, are their stories—the *Outlaw Tales of South Dakota.*

Chief Two Sticks
The Disenchanted Rebel

On a gray midwinter morning just three days removed from Christmas 1894, a crowd gathered round the hastily built gallows in Deadwood Gulch, not to greet the new year or join in good cheer but to witness the end of a once proud life made miserable. On that December day happy holiday hymns were replaced by the woeful death-song wail of a lonely Lakota leader facing the end of his trail. Then, with a hood over his head and a new noose encircling his neck, Chief Cha Nopa Uhah, also known as Two Sticks, stepped onto a small, square trapdoor and dropped seven feet four inches into history.

For the elderly Chief Two Sticks, the previous decades must have seemed as a whirlwind on the prairie, a twister that left no Native American, and perhaps no blade of grass on the Great Plains, unscathed. Two Sticks had witnessed much of what had gone right and so much that had gone wrong for his brethren. Before his death at the end of a white man's rope, he had been first triumphant, then disillusioned, and finally, irrevocably, defeated. That he had walked into old age at all seemed surprising.

For Two Sticks had been at the Greasy Grass with Sitting Bull and Crazy Horse, a day when the clearing of a cloud of smoke and dust coupled with the circling of turkey vultures had signaled the end for Yellow Hair and his band of bluecoats, cut down on the rolling banks of the Little Bighorn. In the years after the battle, he watched with despair as an increasing number of his comrades resigned themselves to a fate dictated by the Great White Father in Washington, reluctantly allowing

1

Studio photo of Chief Two Sticks
Photo courtesy of the Adams Museum

themselves to be assigned to reservations where Indian agents sparingly doled out foodstuffs and government blankets.

One of those Lakota leaders who had never sought surrender was Sitting Bull, with whom Two Sticks had fought at the Little Bighorn. Following the annihilation of Col. George A. Custer and his Seventh Cavalry, Sitting Bull and his followers had fled to Canada. Several years later, hungry and cold, Sitting Bull, his family, and a few remaining warriors surrendered at Fort Buford, North Dakota. Fearing Sitting Bull's influence among his people, the army imprisoned him for two years before allowing him to return to his reservation and people.

The Wounded Knee massacre in December 1890 occurred on the coldest of winter days and left several hundred of his tribe—dozens of unarmed elders, women and children mixed in among them—dead in the snows of a Dakota prairie, shot down by the remnants of the Seventh Cavalry. As the new moons came and went, the loss of his revered friend Sitting Bull and the one-sided "battle" at Wounded Knee still brought a bitter bile to the back of the throat of Chief Two Sticks. The lingering resentment would one day prompt a violent attack on those he viewed as his aggressors that would eventually lead to Two Sticks's death.

For Two Sticks and the remaining rebels of his tribe, and indeed for much of the world, the 1890s were a time of incredible change and challenge. Many whites and Native Americans felt a keen sense of desperation brought on by events they could do little to control. A wave of immigrants had sailed prairie schooners across a sea of grass to settle in the Lakota hunting grounds. In their wake came towns and telegraphs and railroads. In the burgeoning cities and financial centers of the United States, the Panic of 1893 wrought the most serious economic crisis the nation had yet known. Major railroads went bankrupt, followed by a series of bank failures. The National Cordage Company, then the most actively traded stock in the country, went into receivership. At the panic's peak, as much as 18 percent of the U.S. workforce would find themselves unemployed.

The world stage was at least as volatile. On February 15, 1894, French anarchist Martial Bourdin attempted to destroy London's Royal Greenwich Observatory with a bomb, and a month later, fellow anarchist Jean Pauwels died in a Paris church when the bomb he was carrying exploded in his pocket. That summer, French president Sadi Carnot was assassinated by a twenty-one-year-old Italian anarchist who would himself be executed by guillotine less than two months later.

Rebellion was in the air. On March 25 Coxey's Army, the first major American protest march, departed Massillon, Ohio, for Washington, D.C., to bring the plight of the unemployed to national attention. On May 1, as the jobless rioted in Cleveland, some five hundred of populist Jacob Coxey's followers arrived in D.C., where the leaders of the march were promptly arrested for walking on the grass of the U.S. Capitol.

But Two Sticks would have known little of what occurred beyond his personal horizon. His needs were more immediate. His was an existence that required attention to his daily subsistence. With a disdain for reservations and given the virtual extermination of game on the prairies, simply living was his primary focus.

The winter of 1893 found Two Sticks traveling with his two sons, Uses a Fight (or Fights With) and First Eagle, as well as a nephew, Kills the Two, and three more men, No Waters, Hollow Wood, and Whiteface Horses. Together, Chief Two Sticks's band roamed the breaks country of southwestern South Dakota, raiding ranches and stealing cattle.

Known to Indian agents as well as their reservation-bound tribal members, Two Sticks and his band were described by a February 11, 1893, story in the *Black Hills Daily Times* as "Uncompapas," an unflattering term that implied sneakiness and an underhanded approach to their pursuits. The article claimed that Uncompapas were the type of Native Americans who, when in council with other Plains Indians, always positioned themselves near the exit of the circle so they could flee at the first sign of danger. They were, said the newspaper, still nomadic and had remained as uncivilized as they were a quarter of a century earlier.

In early February, under the cover of darkness, Two Sticks and his small party carried out a raid on a herd of cattle belonging to the Humphrey's cattle ranch, located on the White River, a day's ride west of the Pine Ridge Agency. Contracted to raise beef for the growing agency, the cattlemen sent word of the raid to Capt. George L. Brown, the acting Indian agent at Pine Ridge. In turn Brown quickly telegraphed soldiers at Fort Meade, near present-day Sturgis, advising them to remain on alert for further criminal activity. The Eleventh Infantry captain then dispatched half a dozen tribal police officers to apprehend the culprits.

When the tribal officers finally found Two Sticks's encampment, they quickly moved in to make arrests. Two Sticks and his band opened fire. When the dust had settled, five tribal police were dead and the sixth was wounded. Unlike his compatriot Sitting Bull, who had been killed by Indian police, Two Sticks escaped unscathed and invigorated by the brief battle.

The chief and his followers returned to the scene of their earlier crime—the Humphrey ranch—and killed four of the ranchers, later identified as R. Royce, John Bennett, thirteen-year-old Charles Bacon, and sixteen-year-old William Kelly. By some accounts, these four might have been the first white men killed on a reservation since 1876. Two Sticks and his band also exhibited their thirst for revenge by shooting thirty cows and three horses.

Fearing that a full-fledged revolt was in progress, as soon as Captain Brown was informed of the killings, he sent a party of twenty-five Indians commanded by tribal policeman Joe Bush after the murderers. Reports had Two Sticks and his followers holed up at the camp of Young Man Afraid of His Horses. Nineteen years earlier, it had been Young Man Afraid of His Horses who had helped negotiate a treaty that allowed white men to mine for gold in the sacred Black Hills. Although opposed by many of the youngest braves, the treaty undoubtedly ended a bitter debate and curtailed a bloody outbreak of fighting with the whites. His levelheadedness would once again be needed.

While at the camp, Two Sticks purportedly told an Indian man named Crow that the hearts of his young followers were bad, and that during their Ghost Dances, the Great Spirit had advised them to kill the whites for all they had done to exterminate the buffalo and steal that which belonged to the Indians.

When Bush and his tribal troops arrived at the camp of Chief No Waters and Young Man Afraid of His Horses, Two Sticks and his band of warriors refused to surrender and a bloody battle commenced. First Eagle, Kills the Two, and Whiteface Horses were seriously wounded in the initial volley. First Eagle died immediately while Two Sticks was seriously wounded and the others were injured.

As the rebel leader lay bleeding on the ground, Chief No Waters worked his camp followers into a frenzy until they were ready to attack the tribal police. But Young Man Afraid of His Horses intervened and, in an effort to prevent further bloodshed, the peacemaker and his faithful followers positioned themselves between No Waters and his people and the tribal lawmen. When Young Man Afraid of His Horses told No Waters that harming the Indian police in support of murderers would result in all of their deaths, No Waters backed down.

But for Captain Brown the confrontation at No Waters's camp was further evidence that additional bloodshed was probable. Afraid the fight over the apprehension of Two Sticks would incite more violence, Brown gathered more than fifty chiefs at Pine Ridge on February 6, 1893, to discuss the murders and the capture of Two Sticks. During the two-hour meeting, most chiefs agreed that Two Sticks was a troublemaker who was prone to be the first to join insurrectionists. Several chiefs confirmed to Brown that they wanted no part in the hostilities and represented friendly tribes.

Two Sticks's shoulder wound was so serious that reservation officials agreed to hold him at the agency until he was sufficiently recovered to travel to Deadwood for trial. Weeks later, when a U.S. marshal arrived to take Two Sticks to justice, the chief refused to cooperate and encouraged No Waters to protect him. The move gave Two Sticks a one-month reprieve, but when No Waters was arrested, Two Sticks had no recourse but to accompany the marshal to the Black Hills. When he was finally placed in a Deadwood jail, Two Sticks suffered a relapse and remained in guarded condition for several months.

"Two Sticks is wounded in the shoulder, Whiteface Horses in the lower limbs," one observer commented. "Their conditions are loathsome in the extreme. They will not allow a white physician to go near them and their condition can be imagined. Whiteface Horses' legs are gangrened to his knees and his demise is looked for anytime. Two Sticks will probably pull through with the loss of his arm."

Whiteface Horses did later succumb to his wounds. After standing trial on charges of instigating and conspiring to commit murder and resisting arrest, Hollow Wood, No Waters, and Kills the Two were sentenced to five years in jail. Hollow Wood and No Waters would die there, but Kills the Two would serve out his term.

As the leader of the rebel band, Two Sticks would face a different and decidedly more severe penalty. He would be hanged by the neck until dead.

On April 11, 1893, shortly after Two Sticks had been transported to Deadwood, the *Black Hills Daily Times* carried the once-proud Lakota leader's purported confession. It was filled with regrets for the actions of his boys, still maintained his innocence, and showed a measurable amount of remorse that, even at the end, Two Sticks hoped would save him from the gallows.

"My friend I have not much to say for my part," he told a newspaper reporter. "I had nothing to do with the killing of the white men. My son that was killed by the Indian police was the cause of all the trouble. I cannot lie, my boy that is dead killed three of the white men and Whiteface Horses killed the other one. I am going to move away. I want—and die. My boy [Uses a Fight] that is in jail at Deadwood did not have a gun. He had a bow and arrows. He is only eighteen years old and is a coward. My son that is dead had a rifle. Whiteface Horses had a Winchester. The reason we killed them white men did not treat us right. My son said that he wanted to die and be hung."

As he recuperated from his bullet wound, Two Sticks might have wondered at each passing day why a benevolent government would help him heal just so it could put him to death.

At Christmastime, Two Sticks was adjudged to be well enough to be executed and preparations began in earnest. On December 28 all was in readiness and a crowd of curious residents began lurking around the Lawrence County jail yard at 8:00 a.m. By 9:30 those with admission passes were permitted inside an enclosure that consisted of a sixteen-foot-tall solid board fence that spanned the perimeter of the courtyard. At its center stood a solid gallows. By 10:15 two hundred people were packed into the enclosure.

Inside the jail Two Sticks had consumed a last meal of steak grilled over live coals, several slices of bread, and two cups of strong, black coffee. Jailers reported to the assembling press that he had spent his last night sleeping, singing, talking, and walking the floor of his cell. After Two Sticks had finished his meal, Father Florentine Digmann—called "Black Bear" by the Lakota—and W. L. McLaughlin, the condemned's attorney, joined the aging Indian and gently told him that President Cleveland had refused to pardon him for his crimes and that only the gallows and the promise of everlasting life awaited him.

A short time later, a U.S. marshal named Peemiller and a swarm of local dignitaries and reporters walked down the corridor to Two Sticks's cell and the death warrant was read aloud. At first the chief merely grunted. But when asked if he had any reason why the sentence should not be carried out, Two Sticks turned to the marshal and gave it one last try.

"My heart is not bad," he said in a clear voice. "I did not kill the cowboys; the Indian boys killed them. I have killed many Indians, but never killed a white man; I never pulled a gun on a white man. The great father and the men under him should talk to me and I would show them I am innocent. The white men are going to kill me for something I haven't done. I am a great chief myself. I have always been a friend of the white man. The white men will find out sometime that I am innocent and then they will be sorry they killed me. The great father will be sorry, too, and he will be ashamed. My people will be ashamed, too. My heart is straight and I like everybody. God made all hearts the same. My heart is the same as the white man's. If I had not been innocent I would not have come up here so good when they wanted me. They know I am innocent or they would not let me go around here. My heart knows I am not guilty and I am happy. I am not afraid to die. I was taught that if I raised my hands to God and told a lie that God would kill me that day. I never told a lie in my life."

Raising both his hands to the heavens, Two Sticks then began his death song. In it he proclaimed that his heart was good and that God must accept him into his fold when he died. After the chief had gone on for several minutes and had become increasingly emotional, Father Digmann finally quieted him. Two Sticks turned to the clergyman, grasped his hands, and told him he was a good man. His attorney and the marshal also received his favorable attention.

By some accounts Two Sticks was then allowed to meet with his wife, a Chinese woman called China Mary.

"I'm going to die and go to heaven," Two Sticks sadly told her. She replied, "You go to heaven. I'll go to China."

The callousness of his wife's remark may have been too much. According to witnesses Two Sticks grabbed a leather strap from a nearby chair, slipped it around his neck, handed one end to another Indian in the adjacent cell, and began violently jerking against it. Eventually subdued by his white jailers and chastised by Father Digmann, Two Sticks was

9

finally resigned to his fate. He said that he was only trying to ensure that if he died, he did so by the hand of his own people, not the white man's. He then grew calm.

Marshals tied his hands behind his back and the slow march to the gallows began. Two Sticks walked with a firm resolve. As he left the jail and entered the courtyard, he caught his first glimpse of the gallows and the curious onlookers gathered in their death vigil.

Led up steps to the platform, the chief was placed atop a three-foot-square trapdoor. He bowed as the clergyman read a short prayer; then as a hush fell over the courtyard, Chief Two Sticks, who had survived seventy-one winters on the plains, raised his head to the heavens and sang his death song once again. Those present were awed by his steady nerves, even as his executioners placed a noose around his neck and a black hood was pulled over his head.

As time stood still and a lifetime of hunts and heroes undoubtedly passed through Two Sticks's mind, the metallic thump of the trapdoor's mechanism heralded his plunge to death. As the floor fell away, Two Sticks plummeted seven feet four inches until the stout rope reached its end, broke his neck, and killed him instantly. He was left to hang unwavering for fifteen minutes before being declared dead by a quartet of local doctors. Without ceremony the remains of Chief Two Sticks were placed in a coffin and hauled to the local undertaker for burial in an unmarked grave.

Thus ended the long life of a Lakota, caught in a sea of change that he could not navigate.

Madame Vestal

The Lure of Lurline

Madame Vestal began her fabled career as a Confederate spy; parlayed her poise and beauty into lucrative stints at the faro, blackjack, and poker tables of Deadwood in the lawless Dakota Territory; and died downtrodden, forgotten, and lonesome in a San Francisco jail.

Operating as the ears and brains of one of Deadwood's most notorious gangs of stage robbers and vicious murderers, Lurline Monte Verde, as she then called herself, took insider information and transformed it into a prosperous illegal profession. After her exploits were uncovered, she scurried from the Black Hills forever.

They were as desirable as a wool coat in a Dakota ground blizzard, these Wild West women. Lured by the prospect of fortune in the gold camps found throughout the frontier, in places called Deadwood, Virginia City, and Cripple Creek, these women of the plains and pines strived at times just to survive.

Living on the edge of the American frontier—the far edge—was never easy even in the best of circumstances. Nature could be a harsh professor. Friends were found when fortune shined but when times turned tough, one was an orphan. And that was if you were a man.

Somewhere in the mix of emotions that inevitably attends a discussion of women in the Old West resides a wonder at how they survived at all. There were pioneering women, of course, schoolmarms and sodbuster's wives who it is said helped civilize the frayed fringe of these lonely, lawless lands. We all count them among our lineage. But there were also madams and manipulators, hurdy-gurdy harlots and beautiful upstairs girls who could tease, tame, and tap a deep-pocketed prospector faster than he could saddle his horse.

Among the best of these was a woman who had many names but a singular smile. The product of prosperous Southern parents, lovely Belle Siddons was simply that. Shapely, with deep brown eyes and ink black hair, she was born a natural beauty and matured into a stunning woman who could catch any eye. Those ravishing looks would, in turn, lead her to serve as a Confederate spy, lose two husbands, then flee to the gambling parlors of the West. There, on the outskirts of civilization, she would assume many names and secure a lasting reputation as a cunning cardsharp who could read a man as few then could read a book.

Born Belle Siddons around 1840 on a slave plantation in Missouri, she led a life of privilege and class. Her charm, social grace, and beauty—qualities cultivated by her attentive parents—led her to attend the Female University of Lexington, Kentucky. While studying at the university nearly five hundred miles east of her family's estate, Belle earned honors and a measure of independence that would mark the remainder of her life. After graduating, she moved to St. Louis.

Intensely Southern, and armed with an education, upper-class upbringing, and sophisticated appeal, the dazzling debutante was welcomed into virtually every social circle. She became known as the Belle of St. Louis. So alluring was the twenty-five-year-old that when the Civil War broke out in 1861, she successfully worked as a spy for the Confederacy, using her mix of beauty and brains to extract information from unsuspecting Union officers.

But her service as a spy for the South would be short-lived. Arrested in December 1862, tried and convicted for her subterfuge, Belle was sentenced to the Gratiot Street Prison in St. Louis. Gratiot (pronounced grass-shut) was a former medical college positioned in the midst of some of the city's handsomest homes, in which she had been hosted on numerous occasions. Gen. John Charles Fremont's Union headquarters were just a block away in the elegant Brandt Mansion. The wealthy

Harrison family lived just across the street and the Christian Brothers Academy was connected to the prison's north wall.

But moving from the freedoms of fashionable balls and hushed boudoirs to the cell of a Yankee prison must have been unsettling for Belle. The Gratiot Street Prison was used to confine all matter of prisoners. Built for twelve hundred, it housed two thousand, bushwhackers, thieves, and snipers among them. Belle's influential parents did all they could to secure her release, even lobbying a relative who had been governor before the war. Four months following her incarceration, the current, benevolent governor released Belle on the condition that she not return to Missouri for the remainder of the war.

Little is known about how Belle spent the rest of the Civil War and in later life she declined to discuss it, but when Confederate general Robert E. Lee surrendered to General U. S. Grant on April 9, 1865, and President Lincoln succumbed to an assassin's bullet six days later, she returned to Jefferson City and rejoined the social scene. Soon married to Dr. Newt Halleck, a former army surgeon, the two set out for Texas to start their own life. They soon established a private practice, he attending to patients and she serving as his faithful nurse. When the good doctor contracted yellow fever and died, Belle's life changed. Within a year she had remarried, this time to a cardplayer who was devoted to the intricacies of poker, faro, and blackjack. While they were only married for a short time before his early death, she learned from him a love for these games that would last her the rest of her life. All she really needed was a town with easy pickings—places where the law didn't necessarily reside.

After living the high life in a succession of boom-and-bust towns, from Wichita and Fort Hayes to Ellsworth and Cheyenne, the winter of 1876 found the curvaceous cardsharp with a new name and a brand new game in the bustling burg of Denver. Building her stake with a big tent and free beer and whiskey in the shadows of the Rocky Mountains, she was now known as Madame Vestal. The sexual suggestion contained in her new moniker, coupled with an upbringing that wouldn't

Madame Vestal
Illustration by Derek Olson

allow her to employ prostitutes, only added to the allure. Men flocked to her establishment.

As she worked the gaming tables on Colorado's Front Range and summer came to the Rockies, the word of a grand new gold strike filtered down from the Black Hills of Dakota Territory. In places like St. Louis, St. Paul, and Denver, the incredible hunger for gold was so great that some just packed what they and their horse could carry and headed for the hills. Madame Vestal was among them, traveling in an early day "mobile home," a wagon replete with lace curtains, satin pillows, sofa, and cookstove. Following the stage route that ran from Cheyenne to Deadwood, she spent six dusty weeks on the trail, risking the wrath of renegade Indians and brazen highwaymen, before pulling into the muddy and bloody gold-filled gulch known as Deadwood.

In her midthirties and more rambunctious than ever, the arrival of the newly renamed Lurline Monte Verde created such a ruckus that the local newspaper even marked the occasion. According to the *Black Hills Pioneer,* the "sultry and sensuous" Monte Verde was greeted by a throng of dusty miners who lifted the "flawlessly groomed beauty" on their shoulders and paraded her up Main Street amid hoots and hollers and the crack of gunfire.

When she opened the first of several saloons and gaming establishments in Deadwood, Monte Verde quickly proved herself to be a smooth operator. She ran a tight operation, didn't suffer fools, and accommodated nearly everyone in direct proportion to the weight of the gold in their sack. She entertained the likes of Wild Bill Hickok and John Wesley Hardin and sang at the Gem Theatre. She stared down boisterous drunks and matched big bets. It was the stuff of legends. Soon Belle Siddons, alias Belle Halleck, alias Madame Vestal, alias Lurline Monte Verde would take her place beside other, less-attractive femme fatales of the felt, women with names such as Poker Alice and Madame Mustache.

"Thousands who have visited such places as Wichita and Ellsworth the cattle headquarters in Kansas, Cheyenne and Deadwood, will remember seeing this remarkable woman, attired in velvets, lace and diamonds, presiding over a faro table, or sometimes twirling the roulette wheel in the most popular gambling saloons in those cities," the *Deadwood Daily Pioneer-Times* would observe nearly fifty years later. "There she would sit, night after night, month after month, pale, stern and impassive."

She boasted that she had never done a kind act, returned a dollar won, or asked a favor since she became a gambler. She said: "My luck was invariable, and I had a superstition that if I allowed the first thot [*sic*] of kindness to enter my soul it would break the spell. I hated every man who came to play against me: they came to break my bank, why should I spare them?"

With that attitude and daily access to the well-heeled merchants, miners, madams, and professional gamblers common in the still-lawless camp, Monte Verde built alliances, learned lessons, and, finally, became lawless herself. She had help. It arrived in the form of a broad-shouldered, devilishly handsome outlaw named Archie Cummings, the leader of a gang of thieves who robbed stagecoaches by day and gambled by night. That they were better at the former rather than the latter no doubt pleased Monte Verde. She and Cummings soon became lovers.

In her place at the gambling tables and bars of her establishments, Monte Verde was in a prime position to gather intelligence, much as she had done in the Civil War. It was amazing how much one could learn about gold shipments, bank deposits, and stage arrivals if she just listened while other revelers were babbling in a whiskey-induced haze. With the ease of experience, Monte Verde acquired information, then passed it on to her boyfriend for follow-up.

"According to her own confession, [Monte Verde] became the confidante and advisor of the gang," the *Pioneer-Times* reported. "No robbery was undertaken of which she disapproved, and none failed in which she advised and planned the details. Sitting in the gambling hall, quiet and observant each night, she could hear the conversation of all kinds of people. Detectives were lured to her table by 'cappers and steerers' sent out for that purpose, and by her permitted to win money, while she listened to their conversation about road agents. By this means she was enabled to keep the gang posted as to what was going on—when treasure was going to be sent out, or when a gold-laden miner was about to take the stage for the railroad."

As is wont to occur when those with money are involuntarily relieved of it on a regular basis, the Cummings gang's repetitive holdups of stages and shipments leading to and from Deadwood began to cause some consternation. Miners were mad. Bankers were balking. What little law there was smelled a conspiracy.

D. Boone May was just the man to bring outlaws to justice. Tired of having its possessions plundered, Wells Fargo & Co. frequently hired special messengers and fearless gunmen to guard their shipments or to track them when they went missing. Known as a gritty gunfighter who didn't necessarily adhere to the inconveniences of the legal process after capturing a suspect, Boone May just may have been their best. His penchant for letting his gun speak for him would later lead to his indictment for murder and eventual travel to South America, but in 1877 he was hot on the Black Hills trail of the thieves who were robbing local stages.

Suspecting that Lurline Monte Verde was assisting the road agents with inside information and medical assistance, May conned the master scammer into revealing the whereabouts of her outlaw lover. After May telegraphed marshals in Cheyenne, Cummings and two of his associates were arrested boarding a westbound train in Laramie City. They had been headed to San Francisco, where Monte Verde had agreed to meet them. The three road agents were escorted to Cheyenne, then hobbled by leg irons, and sent under guard to Deadwood.

But soon after they crossed the Platte River near Fort Laramie, a party of thirty armed vigilantes stopped the coach carrying the prisoners and made them disembark. The armed men then produced a rope, found a tree, and hanged the captives one by one, using the same rope for each, allowing the last to see the first kick and struggle before suffering the same penalty. Cummings asked permission to pray and write a letter to his mother before he endured the same fate as his friends. The request was granted on the condition that he provide the names of his gang and reveal where he had hidden the loot taken in a succession of holdups. He declined. His captors then offered his life in exchange for his hidden treasure. This he accepted. Once he had provided the location, the vigilantes let him swing from the same tree, then left notice for any passersby to let the body hang.

When Monte Verde learned of her lover's death, she was despondent and turned to liquor. When that didn't deaden the pain, she attempted an overdose with poison. She was unsuccessful in her attempt. But her light was nevertheless snuffed out. She never again shined as brightly.

The one-time belle of the South, sweet spy of the Confederacy, nurse, gambler, saloon keeper, and confederate of robbers and thieves abandoned her characteristic courage, surrendered herself to drink, and dove into the oblivion of Deadwood's Chinese opium dens.

Monte Verde began her last great journey in the fall of 1879 when she took to operating the largest dance hall in Leadville, Colorado. But it was only a wayside rest on the road to eternity. She made other pit stops in Las Vegas, New Mexico, Tucson, and Tombstone, but with each new town she retained her baggage—an overreliance on brandy and opium—and lost money on gambling and bad investments. Her final destination may well have been a cell in San Francisco's city jail.

As promising as her young life was, with all the opportunities and education she was afforded, Belle Siddons, alias Belle Halleck, alias Madame Vestal, alias Lurline Monte Verde, died behind bars in San Francisco in 1881. She was forty-one years old.

Lame Johnny

The Legend of Lost Gold

After a succession of low-budget Black Hills burglaries, horse thefts, and minor stagecoach heists, Lame Johnny and his gang of thieves robbed the Cheyenne & Black Hills Stage Line of gold worth more than $4 million in today's dollars. But they never got to spend it.

When he and his gang were eventually captured, their pockets were empty, literally and figuratively. They never spent the first dime. But where they hid their treasure remains a matter of speculation. The legend of Lame Johnny and his lost gold still lingers in the Black Hills of South Dakota. Indeed, the remains of Lame Johnny still linger there as well—minus his head.

He was born Cornelius Donahue in 1850. His native city of Philadelphia was, at the time, a bustling metropolis of 121,000 residents and the fourth largest city in the United States. Donahue lived there through the Civil War, studied briefly at Girard College, and then headed south to the rangelands of Texas.

As a young man he fell in with the wrong bunch of cowboys, and they saddled him with some bad habits. While working a ranch, he and his fellow cowhands became adept at stealing back the herds of horses that were frequently raided by bands of local Apaches. In short order a horse thief was born.

While some have speculated that polio had left Cornelius with a limp, others have claimed that his awkward gait was the result of a childhood fall from a horse. Whatever the cause, his chosen, albeit illegal, profession as an up-and-coming horse thief required a better moniker than Cornelius. He preferred the alias John Hurley while going about the horse-borrowing business in the Lone Star State, but his physical defect earned him the nickname, "Lame Johnny."

With Texas lawmen closing in on his illegal trade in the 1870s, and with a desire to pursue promising riches over the horizon, Lame Johnny headed north in 1876, following news of a major discovery of gold in the Black Hills of Dakota Territory. Virtually overnight, ramshackle Dakota towns known as Custer City, Hill City, Deadwood, and Lead had sprang up from the forest floor, with hammers banging nails into new boards and six-guns settling disputes.

On a spring day in 1876, Cheyenne freighter John Murphy was preparing to take another load of supplies to Deadwood when he was approached by a mild-mannered man with a noticeable limp who called himself John A. Hurley. The young man inquired about working his way to Deadwood with the freighting outfit and, always in need of help on the dusty, dangerous trail, Murphy readily agreed and found a horse for Hurley.

Days later, when Lame Johnny's wagon train pulled into the wild-and-woolly town of Deadwood, he found himself in the midst of a rough and ribald community where some say there was a death a day—most from unnatural causes. Arriving in Deadwood just a few months before Wild Bill Hickok would play his last hand of poker, the nattily dressed outlaw known as Lame Johnny could just smell the gold being dragged from the ground. Its evidence was everywhere, from new buildings and faro parlors to watered-down whiskey and beautiful upstairs girls. Armed with a new start in a distant place that didn't yet recognize his face, Lame Johnny wanted a taste of it all.

Though some struck it rich panning for gold in the glittering gulches of the Back Hills, Lame Johnny's attempts at prospecting along Castle Creek were less rewarding. The work was laborious and the living conditions difficult. When a band of Lakota braves stole his horses, it may have been the deciding factor in Lame Johnny's decision to take some time away from the legal life and return to his old habits. Drawing on his experiences in Texas, the twenty-six-year-old outlaw borrowed a horse from an acquaintance in Custer City, galloped to the Red Cloud Agency, and stampeded some three hundred Indian ponies north toward the Black Hills. The act led to successive raids on each other's horse herds for the remainder of the summer.

Disappointed by his continuing lack of success in the mining world, Lame Johnny gave up his quest for gold altogether that fall and took a position as a bookkeeper at the Homestake Mine in Lead. While there, he learned about the frequent shipments of gold bullion the company made to far-reaching cities. When someone recognized Lame Johnny as a horse thief who had fled Texas a few steps ahead of the law, he left his job and returned to stealing horses and rustling cattle, eventually advancing to stage robbery.

In his quest for easy money, Lame Johnny joined a ragtag group of loners, losers, and lost souls who found it much simpler to prey on the proceeds of others than to succeed by more legitimate means. One of those fellow outlaws was Jim Fowler, alias Fly Specked Billy, so called because of his face full of freckles. When Fowler later gunned down a patron in a Custer City bar, a lynch mob tied his neck to a tall tree along French Creek and ended his wayward life.

Meanwhile, throughout the late 1870s, Lame Johnny kept up his spree of robbing stages, securing strongboxes, and feeding on the efforts of others. Each time, with posses in pursuit, he and his gang would simply disappear into the forests and ragged ravines of the million-acre wilderness of the Black Hills. Over time, however, Lame Johnny's limp would give lawmen the description they needed to pursue him in earnest.

Two years into his career of Dakota outlawry and seeking the "big score," Lame Johnny would use his inside knowledge of the Homestake's security measures to plan one of the largest heists in Black Hills' history.

The Homestake, which would prove to be one of the longest and most profitable continuously operated gold-mining operations in the world, shipped most of its gold in two-hundred-pound ingots. The practice was designed to discourage stage robbers, as one gold bar could prove to be more than a packhorse could carry. In addition, the company employed a special "treasure coach," called the Monitor, that essentially was an ironclad, portholed fort on wheels carrying cargo and heavily armed guards. Other rifle-wielding sentries on horseback preceded and followed the coach in an effort to protect the prized payloads.

But that didn't deter Lame Johnny and his gang from planning to hold up the Cheyenne & Black Hills Stage Line. When the Monitor made its monthly journey from Deadwood to Cheyenne in October 1878, Lame Johnny's gang was lying in wait. As the stage stopped at Canyon Springs, some thirty-seven miles south of Deadwood, the guards encountered five gunmen with bad intentions. A gunfight erupted and, in the initial confrontation, one of the guards was seriously wounded. As the outlaws closed in on the stage, another guard inside the coach was wounded. Overpowered by the surprise attack, a third guard attempted to flee but was struck down by a bullet and died facedown in the dust.

By some accounts the robbers moved the stage into the woods and spent the next two hours breaking into the strongbox. When the lid was finally lifted, they stared unbelievingly at $3,500 in currency, hundreds of dollars worth of jewelry, $500 in diamonds, and seven hundred pounds of gold dust, nuggets, and bullion. They had struck the mother lode.

The outlaws loaded the gold onto a two-wheeled wagon and scampered away to the east, tracing steep-sided canyons and streambeds to their favorite hideout near Buffalo Gap, on the eastern flank of the Black Hills. Meanwhile, news of the heist spread throughout the region and a reward posted by Homestake sent posses following up on every reported sighting of the fugitives. A month later, with suspect Lame Johnny still on the run, the stage line reported that more than half of the loot had already been recovered. But the getaway wagon and two large gold bars remained missing.

That fall, when Lame Johnny ventured to the Pine Ridge Indian

Reservation to acquire ponies in his customary fashion, he was recognized by a lawman who took him into custody. Transporting Johnny to Chadron, Nebraska, and suspecting him of the Homestake holdup, lawmen took extraordinary measures to ensure his continued captivity while they returned him to Deadwood for trial.

A blacksmith was hired to fashion leg irons for Lame Johnny, which were then riveted to a metal plate fastened to the floor of the stagecoach. Shackled, handcuffed, and escorted by two famed and controversial bounty hunters named Boone May and Frank Smith, Lame Johnny was finally on his way to justice. Accompanying the group was Sheriff "Whispering" Smith and Jesse Brown.

When the stage was some eight miles north of Buffalo Gap, they encountered a group of masked men who stopped their progress. It didn't take the vigilantes long to pry up the metal plate and drag Lame Johnny from the coach. When he wouldn't reveal the location of the hidden gold, it took even less time for them to shoot him, then drag the bleeding and still-shackled body to the nearest elm tree, where they secured a rope around Lame Johnny's neck and lifted him off the ground. There ended the short life of Cornelius Donahue.

The morning after Lame Johnny's early demise, as drovers with Pete Oslund's bull train were moving freight up the same trail, they stumbled upon the scene of Lame Johnny's corpse still swinging from the elm tree. They cut the body down and buried the young man beneath its leafless branches.

Strange rumors of lost heads and Lame Johnny's hidden gold persist to this day. One account had a cowboy cutting off Lame Johnny's head and selling it to a museum. Curious local residents later dug up the grave and discovered Lame Johnny's corpse still shackled, but lacking his cranium. They removed the victim's shackles and boots (one with a high heel for Johnny's deformed foot) and displayed them in local museums and a Buffalo Gap store, respectively. The boots were lost when the store later burned.

Lame Johnny and others in his gang went to early graves without ever revealing the fate of the four hundred pounds of gold bullion they had secreted away from the Monitor stage. Today, that legend of lost gold still captivates treasure seekers and historians alike.

Before it rotted away after decades of exposure to the elements, an epitaph posted on a wooden board above Lame Johnny's grave declared:

Pilgrim Pause!
You're standing on
The molding clay of Limping John.
Tread lightly, stranger, on this sod.
For if he moves, you're robbed, by God.

James Leighton Gilmore

Blood on the Trail

It was a long and dusty trail littered with the discarded hopes of men and the cast-off corpses of oxen that had died along the way. On a fateful day in the spring of 1879, while hauling supplies along the Fort Pierre to Deadwood Trail, James Leighton Gilmore had apparently tired of it all. It didn't seem like his life was going to get any better. Consequently, when a fellow trail driver offered a criticism, Gilmore was in no mood to accept it. He grabbed his revolver, confronted the unarmed antagonist, pulled the trigger, and blew a hole clean through his arm. When the injured man turned to flee, Gilmore leveled his weapon and shot him three more times in the back.

By all accounts James Leighton Gilmore was just attracted to trouble. Despite being the son of prominent residents of Steubenville, Ohio, where his father served as a policeman, young James was a problem child whose mischief would only increase as he got older. Eventually his unruly temper and penchant for agitating authorities, as well as virtually everyone around him, would lead Gilmore to an untimely death at the end of a twisted rope, the first legal hanging in Deadwood, Dakota Territory.

Born in July 1958, the youngest son of a "respected and worthy family," Gilmore was a handful. Late in his young life, his hometown newspaper would use Gilmore's fall from grace as a lesson for youngsters not to follow in his footsteps. "Little boys, pull your chairs up closer and listen to a true story," the *Steubenville Weekly Gazette* reported in its December 22, 1882, edition. "When James Gilmore was a little boy in Steubenville he tried to set the school on fire, shot two horses belonging to a man who had incurred his displeasure, and ran away from home several times. Yesterday he was hanged at Deadwood for murder. That's all children: you can go back to your play."

The *Ohio Press* devoted columns of ink to recounting stories of Gilmore's ill-spent youth. The paper recalled that James was always a wild sort of a boy and was up to all kinds of pranks. He would make out the plans of some piece of devilment, and before that scheme was under way, he would concoct another. He once obtained permission to go out of the schoolroom for a few minutes and then set fire to a pile of paper and shavings in a closet. Returning to the schoolroom he took his seat but hinted to his schoolmates he was up to something. Smoke soon began issuing from the closet, a fire that took several school officials to extinguish. When accused of having started the fire, Gilmore laughed and denied his role in setting the blaze.

The newspaper blamed Gilmore's lack of appropriate behavior not on his respected parents, but on the reading material the young man chose to secret in his bootlegs, about his clothes, and in his school desk. Instead of studying his lessons, Gilmore was prone to peruse the latest in Beadle's dime novels, so much so that at the end of his schooling he apparently couldn't spell his own middle name—Leighton.

His beloved mother died in 1872, when Gilmore was just fourteen years old, giving impetus to the young adventurer and rabble-rouser's plans to explore the West he romanticized. Shortly after his mother's death, Gilmore ran away from home. Searching for an older brother, he found himself in California, but he was unable to locate his sibling. He found work as a drover, herding cattle, a position that undoubtedly took him over many trails, visiting newly built towns, and meeting some of the characters who occupied the West.

Eventually, in 1879, Gilmore found himself working as a mule skinner leading heavily laden oxcarts on the rough and dusty trail between Fort Pierre on the Missouri River and Deadwood, Dakota Territory. Thousands of miners had descended on the Black Hills after Col.

George Armstrong Custer's 1874 expedition had confirmed the presence of gold. Amidst the flurry of thousands of gold seekers and the establishment of new towns and industry came a need for constant resupply. Oxen trains such as the one on which Gilmore worked fed a furious desire for foodstuffs, mining equipment, and other necessities. The parade of wagons across the prairie was so vast that the ruts could still be seen more than a century later.

In the spring of 1879, Gilmore was one of several drivers leading a line of wagons across the Great Sioux Reservation toward Pierre, after having off-loaded provisions in Deadwood. This two-hundred-mile-long trail, before the arrival of railroads, connected the Black Hills to the Missouri River. Horse, mule, and oxen teams carried passengers, supplies, and cargo across the grasslands. Several stage stops and roadhouses were set up along the route. In the late 1870s twenty oxen pulling three wagons with ten tons of freight could make the trip in fifteen days. Depending on the season, it could be extremely hot or outrageously cold work, with men and animals constantly exposed to the elements. Conditions inevitably led to disagreements.

Near Gilmore in the ox train was another mule skinner, a Mexican man named Bicente Ortez, sometimes called Clementi Ortes. Apparently, the two men had been exchanging insults and threats. After driving their teams into camp for the night on the appropriately named Deadman's Creek, the two men began unyoking their animals. While so engaged and in the presence of wagon bosses, an angry Gilmore purportedly said to Ortez, "Now I am going to say right here before the bosses that if you ever scare my cattle again, I'll beef you." Ortez apparently made no reply and continued unyoking his cattle. When finished, the Mexican walked past Gilmore, who offered him a string of profanities. Ortez was equally contemptuous in his retort. Witnesses later recounted that Gilmore said, "You wait a bit and I'll fix you."

As Ortez walked away and sat down on a yoke to rest after the long day's haul, Gilmore went to his wagon, took out a revolver, buckled the holster around him, and walked back to where Ortez was sitting with his back to the gunman. Swearing, Gilmore cocked his revolver and told Ortez to defend himself. As Ortez started to rise from his perch, Gilmore shot the defenseless man in the left arm, below the shoulder. Seriously injured by the first volley and having no weapon himself, Ortez attempted to flee, but Gilmore fired three more shots, striking the Mexican in the back, the bullets penetrating and passing entirely through his body.

As the smoke cleared and Ortez lay writhing on the ground, Gilmore casually turned and walked out of the corral, intending to escape back to the still-lawless Black Hills. The wagon boss picked up a gun, confronted Gilmore, and told him to drop his weapon, which he did, but then continued on in his attempted escape. Three of the other men then armed themselves and set out after Gilmore, who was on foot. They found him wandering half a mile from camp. After escorting him back, and in one of those curious frontier customs in which the law is less respected than the camaraderie of a fellow trail driver, the men then took up a collection of $18 for him, gave him a horse, and sent him on his way.

In agony from his wounds, the "Mexican Ortez," as newspapers would later describe him, lingered until nine o'clock the next morning, when he drew his last gasp. He was buried not far from the trail, under a small stone marker, not far from an intermittent tributary that would become known as Mexican Creek.

While Ortez lay dying, Gilmore rode to Pierre and hid out for four or five days. He then steered his mount along the Missouri to the territorial capital of Yankton, before turning west for the Rosebud. Hoping to hide out on the Indian reservation, Gilmore soon found work as a bullwhacker, driving mules for the government. When deputy marshals caught up to him months later, Gilmore had found more gainful employment running a saloon variously called Three Mile Ranch and Hog Ranch.

Taken into custody for the long ride to Deadwood, Gilmore asked Deputy Marshal Gray why he was being arrested. "Is it for killing that son of a bitch Mexican?" He added, "That was an accident. I only intended to wing him." Three bullets in the back might have argued otherwise.

Gilmore's arrival in Deadwood caused quite a twitter. After all, no one had been legally hanged in the town since it was born, although many had been honored guests at necktie parties thrown by enthusiastic vigilantes. But along with this man's arrival on charges that carried the most severe of penalties also came the first real test for the authority of the territorial government.

In mid-August, the man known then as James Leighton was assigned attorneys and placed in the county jail, a ramshackle building so insecure that his captors were forced to put the prisoner in leg irons and shackle him in a metal cage. He would stay there for more than two years while his case awaited trial, his conviction was appealed and upheld by the Supreme Court of Dakota Territory, and, finally, all other imaginable appeals were exhausted.

When a jury was impaneled on September 5, 1881, two years after the killing occurred, witnesses described an incident on the Fort Pierre to Deadwood Trail in which a young, hot-tempered trail driver shot and killed another bullwhacker, then fled the scene. The defense, in turn, argued that Ortez had threatened on several occasions to kill Gilmore, that the Mexican was bad, and that Gilmore had shot him only when he thought Ortez was reaching for his knife. As the newspaper reported, "[t]his story was not confirmed in any particular way by those who were eyewitnesses to the homicide."

When it was time for closing arguments, Gilmore's attorney claimed the shooting amounted to the justifiable homicide of a mean-spirited Mexican teamster who had threatened Gilmore's life. Conversely, according to the *Daily Times*, the prosecutor, Hugh J. Campbell, "told them that in this land of the free, every man, regardless of color, creed, or other station in life was equal before the law, and the law protected with its folds, the plebian as well as the millionaires, and it knows no difference between the bull-whacker and the bonanza king."

When Campbell concluded the prosecution's case on September 7, Judge J. C. Moody charged the jury and sent them out for deliberations. But their minds were made up. Within minutes they returned a verdict of guilty of murder as charged. As jailers led him away, Gilmore's only comment was aimed at an officer of the court, to whom he angrily said that if the officer didn't think he could take his medicine like a man, he was dead wrong.

Two weeks after his conviction, which carried a mandatory penalty of death by hanging, Gilmore's attorney filed his first appeal. A week later the *Black Hills Daily Times* published a poem purportedly penned by Gilmore, in which he lamented the loss of a mother's love. The poem created a stir, second thoughts in some, and cynicism in others. "He is full of hell all the time as he ever was," remarked one insider, "and dances a double clog and sings every day."

On October 20 the Dakota Territory Supreme Court extended Gilmore's heavily mortgaged lease on life by agreeing to consider his appeal in its May 1882 term. Just five days later, the *Daily Times* reported on the disturbing conditions of the county jail and what Deadwood's star prisoner had been up to. Under the headline, ARRANGING FOR LIBERTY, it stated:

> The jail of Lawrence County is a log ramshackle affair that never can be made secure. To place a prisoner in a dark dungeon, which is the only secure place in the jail, would be cruel, therefore all that can be done is to shackle and chain prisoners convicted of capital crimes. In spite of all the vigilance of the jailers prisoners can receive aid from outside friends. For a few days past the authorities have been satisfied something was going on wrong. A search was made and in Leighton's cell two files were found. Leighton had filed his shackles down thin, and in a short time would doubtless have made a break for liberty. The place is expensive and insecure.

When the condemned man's brother, an attorney, arrived in Deadwood in late October, authorities learned that James Leighton was in fact, James Leighton Gilmore. Fred Gilmore spoke with his brother's attorneys about entering a plea of insanity for him. He claimed James had "always shown symptoms of looseness in the mental machinery," a condition that he said was in some degree hereditary. However, in reporting this, the newspaper noted that the high court could only consider evidence that had been presented at trial.

Fred Gilmore headed east to seek a pardon directly from U.S. president Chester A. Arthur, a fifty-year-old Episcopalian lawyer and teacher who had assumed the presidency just two months earlier after the assassination of President Garfield. Over the next few months, as the lawyer Gilmore sought to penetrate the Washington bureaucracy, convict Gilmore was the recipient of numerous jailhouse visitors. Newspaper reporters just couldn't get enough of him. Leading homemakers and businessmen stopped for a chat, and some thought twice about how this congenial twenty-two-year-old man could have possibly charted a course that led him to this hateful place.

In the newspaper Gilmore was transformed from a cold-blooded killer into "the unfortunate young man now confined . . . under sentence of death. The prisoner is a young man, well built, with rather a handsome face, and a decidedly frank and engaging manner."

When the U.S. Supreme Court convened in May, justices considered Gilmore's claims of self-defense. But in a five-page ruling issued that summer in which each of the justices concurred, they discounted all Gilmore's appeals, saying proof of prior threats against Gilmore by Ortez were not material because, at the time of his death, Ortez was unarmed and was not threatening Gilmore.

On July 18, 1882, Gilmore found himself back in court for what was billed as the second and final sentence of death to be delivered by Judge Moody. Looking thin and pale, Gilmore could only watch as his attorney's motion for a new trial was overruled and the judge set the hanging for September 8, between the hours of 10:00 a.m. and 4:00 p.m. When the newspaper visited Gilmore in his cell ten days later, they found him cleanly shaven with "the look of a boy nineteen or twenty years old." A few days later, Gilmore's brother reported from Washington that the U.S. attorney general would be recommending a commutation of the sentence to life in prison. It was wishful thinking. At about the same time, the U.S. marshal's office received word that the president had elected to let the law take its course.

Nonetheless, appeals also had been delivered to Dakota Territory's governor, Nehemiah Ordway. His consideration further delayed the execution when, finally on November 7, he gave Gilmore's advocates ten days in which to finalize their appeals. The last-ditch effort generated sympathies for the condemned man, statements in the newspaper saying locals now favored life in prison to death, and "prominent and highly respected ladies" were circulating petitions on Gilmore's behalf.

On November 15 Gilmore's last hope for a reprieve vanished when a dispatch was received from a U.S. marshal in Yankton stating that the president would not intercede and that officials in Deadwood should prepare for the hanging of James Leighton Gilmore. The next day, a letter to the editor appeared in the *Daily Times*, calling for mercy.

"In our county jail lies a young man, only 24 years of age, under a death sentence," the letter stated. "In his early youth his mother died. Thus deprived of her gentle love and sweet influence—but for whom a Christian mother can deeply plant and nurture the seeds of honor, love and truth—at the age of 14 he wandered from home and was unfortunately thrown among reckless and dissipated men. He saw the unprincipled succeed—men who constantly disobeyed every moral law, and trampled upon every social courtesy, escaped the law. The filthy and pernicious books with which our news depots abound, were at his disposal. In the midst of all these corruptions, what wonder that he fell! Let the voices of our citizens—of all the citizens of these Black Hills be as a unit—appeal to our governor this day for a stay of this death sentence,

Gilmore gravesite
Photo by T. D. Griffith

the first execution in this beautiful and prosperous country. Fathers, pause in your busy hours and think of that aged father, bowed down by grief and anguish. Mothers, pray for him. His mother is not here to plead for her son's life. Her voice is stilled—she is dead! Therefore, let it not be." The letter was signed, simply, "A Mother."

The same day, Governor Ordway stayed the execution until Friday, November 24. Then two days before that fateful date, the governor again delayed the execution, this time until mid-December. Despite the continued appeals and stays, this would prove to be the last concession by authorities.

In a lengthy story that ran in the *Daily Times* on December 15, published under the headline, AT LAST: A FULL AND GRAPHIC ACCOUNT OF THE FINAL FALL, the newspaper noted that anyone who could read was familiar with the case of James Leighton Gilmore and that Gilmore had never denied that he was guilty of killing Ortez. The newspaper then carried the young man's final words, made while standing on the sturdy gallows, surrounded by a throng of onlookers.

"I have to say gentlemen here, that I was fetched here by my own fault," Gilmore said in a loud, clear voice. "I don't know what is the reason, but when I was small I always had a bad temper. I was not such a wayward child, but I was born with a desire to ramble all the time. Before my mother died I think I was a good child in everything. She died when I was young, and after that I did not appear to have much pleasure at home. My father was a man willing, perhaps, to do everything to take care of me, but I wanted to wander away from home and left home three or four times, and my father fetched me back, and I went to California. Still my heart has not been bad.

"I killed this Mexican, and he is the only man I ever killed. I did not shoot another man, but I did not want to kill him or anything like that. The gun went off accidentally when I was fooling with it. I have only to say this—I put my trust in God. I know I have been bad. I put my trust in God, even now, if it is too late. I put my trust in God. That is all."

But it wasn't. Following another prayer, Gilmore spoke up once again. "I wish to say I have no hard feelings toward anyone. It is the saying I have been a man to kill people, but it is not in my heart. Everybody felt hard against me; but I have not been that kind of man at all. And I can only ask God to let death be short and speedy. That is all I can ask. Father, receive and forgive me as thou didst the thief on the cross. Good-bye, Fa—"

In midsentence the trapdoor gave way and Gilmore fell seven feet, his last request honored by a broken neck and instant death.

Bud Stevens

Acquitted of Murdering a Cattle King's Son

Dode MacKenzie had the world at his feet when he walked into a LeBeau, South Dakota, bar in December 1909. The son of a millionaire cattle baron living in a time when a million dollars meant something, Dode was as handsome as he was cocky. And some just didn't take too kindly to that. Even so, when he was gunned down by a bully of a bartender, it heralded a new legend and signaled the end of a small town.

In the late 1800s and early 1900s, fueled by foreign investment and millions of acres of belly-high sweetgrass, Texas cattlemen began moving massive herds to the outback of South Dakota, Montana, and Canada. In a few short decades, cattle blackened the plains as the bison once had. One of the major operators, the Matador Land and Cattle Company, had begun modest operations in Texas in 1878 with a herd of eight thousand head. However, as English and Scottish investors poured money into capital stock, the Matador benefited from low expenses, good grass, and high beef prices and blossomed. By 1882 when Scottish investors incorporated the company, it had a value of $1.25 million and held ownership of 100,000 acres of rangeland, privileges to another 1.5 million acres, 40,000 head of cattle, and 265 horses.

In 1890 Murdo MacKenzie became manager of the Matador, upgraded the herd, and began leasing northern pastures for maturing the company's purebred steers. He would later be labeled "the most influential of American cattlemen," by President Theodore Roosevelt. Under MacKenzie's guidance the Matador secured five hundred thousand acres of rangeland on South Dakota's Cheyenne River Indian Reservation and three hundred thousand acres on the Pine Ridge Indian

Reservation. He acquired nearly one million more acres in Montana, Texas, and Saskatchewan, Canada.

Born in County Ross, Scotland, on April 24, 1850, MacKenzie received an education, worked as an apprentice in a law office and served a decade as an assistant factor for the Balnagown Estate of Sir Charles Ross. In 1876 he married Isabella Stronach MacBain and the couple had five children. In 1885 MacKenzie became manager of the Prairie Cattle Company in Trinidad, Colorado, where he moved his growing family. Six years later, he was offered the manager's position at the prestigious Matador Land and Cattle Company.

As the Matador's vast operations grew, MacKenzie had the opportunity to assign his sons select positions within the company. For son David George MacKenzie—"Dode" to his friends—the assignment came in north central South Dakota. Thanks to the Matador, the tiny town of LeBeau had become one of the largest cattle shipping points in the United States. A snub-nosed ferry boat shuttled back and forth across the muddy Missouri, hauling cattle from the western ranches to the LeBeau terminal for rail shipment east. Cattle herded from Texas, New Mexico, and Colorado also were fattened up on the fertile range-lands before being shipped to market.

Despite its later success LeBeau had extremely humble beginnings. Established in 1875 by French fur trader Antoine LeBeau, it initially served as a trading post on the east bank of the Missouri near the mouth of Swan Creek, some seventy miles upstream from Pierre. As sod-busters flocked to the prairie, LeBeau grew, and by the early 1880s, the town had 250 residents and 60 buildings.

But with the arrival of the Matador herds in 1907, LeBeau witnessed its own renaissance. As the central shipping point, LeBeau enjoyed a surge in commerce but also had to cope with the law-enforcement challenges that came with this success. As dusty cowpunchers assembled with enough pay in their pockets to gamble freely, raise a little hell, and drink enough to drown out the taste of the trail, saloons, hotels, and bawdy houses were soon catering to all these new customers.

One of LeBeau's most frequent and popular visitors was Dode MacKenzie. After leaving college and following in his father's footsteps, he spent a season working cattle in the Texas Panhandle, then came north to the Cheyenne pastures in the summer of 1909. The *Mobridge Tribune* would later describe him as tall, rugged, and handsome, "a man's man" adored by women, but who preferred hanging out with cowboys in a saloon to a stodgy social life. LeBeau's deputy sheriff admitted that a nick in his ear came while Dode was shooting out lights in a honky-tonk. Dode also reportedly shot at the heels of dancing girls in another joint.

Manager of the Matador's herds on the Cheyenne River Indian Reservation, Dode was often described as lacking his father's reserve. Strident, hotheaded, and a heavy drinker, Dode quickly made a name for himself in a town whose officials often looked the other way in view of the MacKenzie family's power over the northern range and the prosperity the Matador had brought to LeBeau. But that too would change.

The summer of 1909 brought a cattle season unlike any other. That fall, more than 150,000 head were loaded on boxcars at LeBeau, destined for eastern markets. Money flowed as freely as the watered-down whiskey served in the local saloons, such as the most popular run by one-eyed Phil Dufran. Former Matador employee Benjamin F. "Bud" Stevens, also called Stephens and Stephenson, now manned the bar at Dufran's saloon, and he and Dode had a history of bad blood that went back all the way to Texas.

When Dode rode into LeBeau on the morning of December 11, 1909, trailed by a bunch of his cowboys, all of them were intent on quenching their thirst and celebrating a great season. Those with Dode said he got a bit boisterous, but he didn't have a drink and wasn't looking for trouble. Later testimony would contradict this version, however, claiming that Dode was gunning for Stevens and that the bartender had been informed of that fact and had armed himself accordingly. "To spice the monotony of a dull Saturday morning some town punks told

Bud Stephens he had better have his gun ready as Dode MacKenzie was coming in to get him," according to the *Walworth County Record*, published in nearby Selby, South Dakota. "So Bud had his gun in easy reach when Dode came in the door just before noon."

At about 11:30 a.m. on that Saturday morning, the thirty-one-year-old Dode sauntered into the saloon accompanied by two of his cowboys, Walter MacDonald and Ambrose Benoist. Behind the bar stood an agitated Stevens, a fifty-five-year-old man who had been discharged in Texas by the Matador. Dode and his boys walked to the bar, where an argument ensued between Stevens and the rancher. When Stevens taunted Dode, the younger man told the bartender he would have no trouble with him in the bar, but if he, Stevens, would like to take it up on the street outside, Dode would only be too happy to oblige.

Stevens's response was immediate and extreme. Retrieving a cocked .45-caliber Colt from beneath the bar, he aimed it straight at Dode MacKenzie's chest and pulled the trigger. "Dode crossed his arms over his chest, turned and started toward the door when another shot was fired," an eyewitness told the newspaper. "The bullet entered the left arm, went through the body and grazed the right arm. Before Dode reached the door he was shot again in the back. He stumbled out of the door, half-circled on the sidewalk, then fell to the ground."

Friend Jack Wilson was the first to reach him. "Did he hit you, Dode?" Wilson asked. "Yes, he did," came a faint reply. Fred Richmond took one look at the downed cowboy and said, "My God! Dode is dying." Hearing Richmond make the remark, Dode reached his hand out to him, which Richmond grasped. With three bullets lodged in his body, Dode gasped, "Oh! Oh!" and was gone.

A doctor, C. L. Olson, arrived and quickly realized Dode's condition extended beyond his area of expertise. Three decades later, Olson would still remember that historic day. "When Dode MacKenzie was killed I was just across the street in my office and I reached him just as he had collapsed on the sidewalk, being aroused by the shooting," Olson had said in a later interview. "With another man, I do not recall his name, I rendered what service was indicated. He was beyond all help and was unable to make any statement."

When it was clear Dode was dead, Matador cowboys gingerly scooped up the body of their boss and took him to a nearby house. A coroner was called, telegraphs were dispatched, a box was secured, and the friends of Dode MacKenzie, who one would suspect would be hankering for a lynching, instead respectfully attended to the young man's remains. There would be time enough for justice.

Shortly after the shooting, a Deputy Sheriff Peterson had visited Dufran's saloon, arrested Stevens, and secured the pistol with which Stevens had killed Dode. Enlisting the aid of town leaders, the deputy had Stevens held while he found a team and a wagon to transport him to the county seat of Selby.

In the wake of the violence, messages were sent to Murdo MacKenzie, Dode's father, and to James Burr, bookkeeper at the Matador Ranch. The elder MacKenzie left at once for LeBeau, but when it became apparent he would not reach the town in time for the coroner's inquest, he instead arranged for a special train to convey the remains of his boy back to Colorado.

On Sunday, a day after Dode's death, a Sheriff Hoven and U.S. Attorney Smith arrived in LeBeau and interviewed witnesses. That night, in his Selby jail cell, Stevens was informed for the first time that Dode had died. "When he was told, he turned ghastly pale and for the first time appeared to be deeply moved."

A few days later, a coroner's inquest was held and witnesses described details of the tragedy. The coroner's jury found that MacKenzie came to his death at the hands of Stevens and recommended the suspect be remanded to circuit court for trial. Held without bail, Stevens quickly hired attorneys P. C. Morrison of Mobridge and E. B. Harkin of Aberdeen to defend him against the charges.

Two days after Christmas 1909, and just two weeks after the murder,

Stevens found himself in court for his preliminary hearing. Testimony left no doubt that he had shot Dode MacKenzie and that he would be using an argument of self-defense when they went to trial. He wouldn't have to wait long.

On Tuesday, March 22, 1910, Stevens went on trial in Selby for the murder of the cattle king's son. Jury selection was made in one day and the prosecution completed its case the next. On Thursday the defense began presenting a long list of witnesses to prove that MacKenzie had made threats against the aging Stevens, and that Dode had purchased a gun shortly before the shooting. On Friday both sides made closing arguments, with prosecutors calling for justice for the deceased. When it was defense counsel's turn, Harkin "delivered the most comprehensive and logical argument that has ever been presented here," the *Walworth County Record* reported. "His words impressed the jury and at times tears rolled from the eyes of some of them."

The case was given to the jury at 11:00 a.m. Saturday. After four hours of deliberation, they were back with their verdict: not guilty. When informed of the verdict, Stevens was overcome with emotions and silently shook the hand of each of those on the jury.

Freed by authorities but still fearing retribution from Dode's friends, Stevens fled to Mobridge, where he was still in hiding a week later. But the real reckoning for the demise of Dode MacKenzie would come soon and involve the fate of more than one man; it would sound a death knell for an entire town.

After burying his handsome son, Murdo MacKenzie (for whom the town of Murdo, South Dakota, would be named) set about burying a whole community. For the acquittal of Bud Stevens, the Matador outfit immediately boycotted LeBeau and soon ceased all operations on the Cheyenne River Indian Reservation. As the town dried up, so did the revenues of the Chicago, Milwaukee, and St. Paul Railroad and it soon abandoned plans to bridge the river and lay track westward.

In the summer of 1910, just four months after Stevens walked free, a raging fire burned more than half of the buildings on LeBeau's Main Street. All evidence pointed to arson. Fire hoses throughout the small town had been cut and flammable chemicals were discovered in the smoldering walls of burned-out buildings.

Cattle baron Murdo MacKenzie would live another three decades following his son's untimely death, serving as founding president of the American Stock Growers Association and managing a Brazilian cattle operation before ultimately returning to Denver and once again leading the Matador. He died on May 30, 1939, and was buried in Denver.

Had Murdo MacKenzie lived longer, he may have gained some perverse satisfaction in knowing that the charred remains of the town he blamed for the death of his son would one day be hidden beneath the silent waters of Lake Oahe, formed as a result of a flood control project on the Missouri River.

Charles Brown

Savage Killer Swings by His Neck

Following a night of heavy drinking, poker playing, and running up substantial losses, Charles Brown quietly sliced the screen door of his former employer's business, lifted the latch, slipped into the popular Deadwood restaurant, and began searching for valuables. As he entered the bedroom of Mrs. Emma Frances Stone, at the back of the restaurant, in the dead of night, he heard her soft snoring and saw her small dog sleeping on the bed next to her.

Drunk and broke, Brown tried to jimmy the lock of a trunk within which he knew the woman stored valuables. When his pocketknife proved ineffective, he returned to the kitchen and retrieved a butcher knife and a meat cleaver. As he tried to pry open the top of the trunk, the small dog began to growl. Fearful it would awaken Mrs. Stone, Brown grabbed the animal and snuffed out its life before it could bark. When the commotion roused the woman, Brown struck a single savage blow with the meat clever that hit Mrs. Stone above the bridge of her nose and nearly cleaved her head in half. Panicked, the killer threw a pillow over the slain woman's head; nabbed a gold watch, some jewelry, and coins; and fled the establishment.

As he left the scene of the grisly murder, Brown woke his seventeen-year-old grandson by marriage, Ralph Walker, who was sleeping in a room nearby, and the two hopped into Brown's wagon and rode in darkness to his home near Whitewood.

When the sun rose about 5:15 on the morning of May 16, 1897, it signaled the start of the day for waitress Maggie Hudson. Her first customer was Leon J. Libby, and he wanted eggs with his meal. The order

42

required that Maggie retrieve the eggs from storage in the small apartment where her boss, Mrs. Stone, often slept while her husband was out of town. Not wishing to awaken her employer at such an early hour, Maggie quietly opened the door and entered the room. The bloody scene she encountered made her flee for help.

Scurrying back to the dining room, Maggie asked Mr. Libby to confirm her suspicions. "Libby then entered the storeroom and a short investigation soon satisfied him that Mrs. Stone was dead and had been murdered," the *Deadwood Weekly Pioneer* reported on May 20, 1897. "Hastily leaving the room he told Miss Hudson to allow nobody to enter and then went out in search of a policeman."

When informed of the crime, Chief M. J. Donovan and Sheriff Matt Plunkett immediately suspected Ralph Walker and Charles Brown, the latter of whom had recently left the employ of Mrs. Stone. Both Brown and Walker were black, so the police were perhaps racially motivated in directing attention to the two men. but both had also been seen leaving town in Brown's wagon in the early morning hours of the murder. Without delay three law officers headed for Brown's house, where they found and arrested the two men without incident, handcuffed them together, and transported them back to Deadwood.

To law enforcement officers Charles Brown was a known commodity. A year earlier, they had arrested the man for what today would be described as a domestic dispute, but which in the latter part of the nineteenth century was treated far differently by the press. In a sad display of journalism, the *Daily Pioneer Times* of Deadwood used racial epithets to report on February 6, 1896, that Charles Brown had "amused himself Saturday night" by "thumping" the Chinese woman with whom he was living. And when the court ruled on the matter a few days later, the newspaper stated, "The evidence was positive against Brown, and he was fined $15 for the fun he had Saturday night . . ."

As news of the vicious murder of Mrs. Stone spread through the Deadwood community, it set off a wave of recriminations against

Charles Brown
Photo courtesy of the Adams Museum

Brown and his suspected accomplice. When it was learned that law enforcers were returning the suspects to Deadwood, the cry of lynching went up and the townsfolk demanded revenge.

Forewarned about the potential vigilantes, the sheriff elected to split the suspects up. He placed Brown in the custody of a deputy and deputized four other trustworthy men on the spot. He kept custody of the teenaged Walker and led the suspect right through town to the jail without incident. Meanwhile, the five deputies with Brown took a more circuitous route to the jail, staying to the backstreets and railroad tracks. As they closed in on downtown, they encountered small bands of men with hate in their eyes.

"Only a short distance had been gone when the posse found itself confronted by a mob of several hundred," according to the *Times*'s account. "Cries of 'hang him!' 'get a rope' and other like expressions, indicative of the temper of the crowd, were heard on all sides."

But the honorable men selected by the sheriff were not to be deterred in their mission. "It was then that the officers drew their weapons, and on a double-quick hustled Brown into jail," said the *Times*. "Even after they had been locked up, the mob continued to linger about the jail and courthouse, apparently only waiting for someone to take the lead and make a rush to get at the prisoners."

As the excitement died and the mob disbanded, law officers began gathering evidence in the crime. Police identified and arrested eight "colored" witnesses, as the *Times* reported, and others as possible accomplices and jailed them all. Doctors examined the victim's body and determined the death had been caused by wounds inflicted with a sharp instrument such as an ax. Workers at the restaurant noticed that a large cleaver and carving knife were missing from the kitchen. A search of the creek bed closest to the murder scene yielded a meat clever and a butcher knife.

While Brown sat in jail awaiting arraignment, he must have pondered how the course of his life had brought him to his present predicament.

Brown was born a Missouri slave on March 1, 1843, the property of a Colonel Halliday. Brown's mother died when he was nine, and the young man was sold to a neighboring slaveholder with a brutal overseer. As an eighteen-year-old, Brown had witnessed the start of the Civil War and when he was nineteen, President Lincoln issued the Emancipation Proclamation. But as he lived in a Confederate state that denied him and his fellow slaves any measure of freedom, the war and proclamation meant relatively little to Brown.

In the midst of the Civil War, Brown, now twenty years old, was sent to St. Louis, sold to a Frenchman, and had his name changed to Isadore Cavanaugh. After accompanying his owner to California, Brown became a freeman. Brown's release from his master meant independence and adventure. He traveled to Portland, Oregon, then sailed around South America's Cape Horn to New York City while working on a merchant vessel. He signed on as a servant to a Captain Taylor, a cavalryman, and accompanied him across the Atlantic Ocean to Liverpool, England, before returning to New York.

Brown's exploits took him to Chicago, New Orleans, and Mexico, before he found steady work as a cattle driver in Texas. On his final drive Brown found himself at Fort Randall, on the Missouri River in Dakota Territory. He married in March 1872 at age twenty-nine, then settled in Sidney, Nebraska, before seeking work five years later in Wyoming and Colorado. By 1879, three years after its settlement, Brown and his wife were living in Deadwood, where he would stay for the remainder of his days.

When his wife left him, Brown was devastated, and he spiraled downward, living what he later admitted to a newspaper reporter was "not a righteous life." He had frequent run-ins with the law; they culminated in his arrest for the cold-blooded murder of Mrs. Emma Stone, wife of Col. L. P Stone.

While Brown contemplated his crime behind bars, the citizens of the Black Hills paid their respects to the family of his victim, filling a local church for the funeral and singing soulful hymns that included "Asleep in Jesus," "Nearer My God to Thee," and "Shadow of a Mighty Rock." "The sobs and groans of the husband and daughter filled each heart present with grief and sorrow so intense as to be almost beyond description, and the thoughts that went out toward the author of the cause of their agony were bitter ones," the *Deadwood Weekly Times* reported on May 20. The account went on to describe the attack on Mrs. Stone as a "terrible, cowardly, cold-blooded tragedy."

When Brown was finally arraigned in circuit court before Judge A. J. Plowman, newspaper reporters were aghast that the "negro" defendant didn't just plead guilty and expedite the entire judicial process. As it would eventually play out, it was quick enough. "The courtroom was crowded, as the report had been going that Brown, the accused, was going to plead guilty, thereby merely devolving upon the court the unpleasant task of passing sentence," the *Times* noted. "A sense of disappointment was predictable when the ebony-hued suspect said, 'not guilty.'" Judge Plowman set trial for June 10, a scant twenty-six days after the crime had taken place.

With W. L. McLaughlin and Thomas E. Harvey appointed as his counsel, the trial of Charles Brown began June 10, with jury selection and without a single challenge from the defense. The *Times* noted the next day, "It was plain to be seen, then, that the defense did not intend to pursue a vigorously fought case."

Although no one had actually witnessed the crime, prosecutors left little doubt of who had performed the dastardly deed. In sobbing testimony the victim's husband identified his dead wife's gold watch, as well as the knife and cleaver purportedly used in the murder. "It was a pathetic scene and there were but few dry eyes in the vast audience," the *Times* stated. "Brown was not affected in the least, however, but sat as unconcerned and indifferent as could be."

Walker gave damaging testimony against his grandfather, but the government's star witness turned out to be Lead police chief Thomas J.

Sparks. He told the court that Brown had called him to his jail cell the Wednesday prior to the trial and made a full confession, exonerating all others still implicated in the crime. With Sparks's testimony completed, the trial was handed over to defense attorney Harvey.

"Mr. Harvey arose and the courtroom was hushed to breathless silence, while the suspense was intense," according to the June 17 *Deadwood Weekly Pioneer.* "The defendant's counsel had not offered any evidence, had made but one objection to evidence submitted by the state and not more than three or four witnesses were cross-examined."

The defense attorney then thanked the court and the citizens of South Dakota for their concern and courteous treatment. In light of the defense's submission, prosecutors cut short their closing remarks and Judge Plowman charged the jury and sent them out for deliberations. They were back in twenty minutes. The verdict, unsurprising to even the defendant, was guilty of murder as charged and fixing the penalty at death.

On his final day of life, Brown approached his impending death with surprising calm, grace, and dignity. In a statement by him published by the *Times* on July 14, the date of his execution, Brown apologized for his crime, affirmed his renewed faith in God, and asked for forgiveness. "I have admitted to man, and before God, that I have killed Emma Frances Stone," he wrote in his final statement. "I am sorry of it, and of all my sins I ask God to forgive me. I feel that He has forgiven me, and now that I have admitted the truth to man, I feel satisfied in the strength of the Lord Jesus Christ to depart from this world as a Christian."

After a breakfast of toast and eggs, a prayer with a Catholic priest, and a last smoke on his favorite pipe, Brown walked firmly into the crowded courtyard clutching a crucifix. After a final prayer, the condemned man was asked if he had anything to say.

After Brown's hands and legs were strapped and a black cap was pulled over his head, the noose was adjusted around his neck. At 10:29 a.m., Sheriff Plunkett pulled the lever and Brown dropped six feet to his death.

Wild Bill Hickok

Jack McCall Claimed the Life of a Legend

James Butler Hickok had traveled to Deadwood in the summer of 1876 to mine for a glittery metal that would make life easier for him and his new wife. Before he arrived, glowing reports had echoed from the Black Hills of Dakota Territory. Gold nuggets lay on every hillside. Gold dust could be found clinging to the shallow roots of prairie grasses. It was, they said, the new El Dorado.

But three weeks after arriving amidst the mud and blood that was the bustling burg of Deadwood, Wild Bill, as his friends called him, found himself most commonly at a poker table in a dimly lit saloon. To compound his woes, he was losing. He had entered Lewis, Nuttall & Mann's No. 10 Saloon shortly after noon on Wednesday, August 2, 1876, in search of drinks and entertainment. He was to find something much different.

A half dozen people were in the popular saloon and gaming hall when Wild Bill arrived, including Carl Mann, co-owner of the establishment. Charlie Henry Rich, whom Bill knew from his time in Cheyenne, Wyoming, was shuffling the deck, while former Missouri River boat captain William Massie awaited his cards. Thinking he'd join them for some draw poker, Wild Bill asked Charlie Rich if he could have his seat, as the back of the chair was against the wall, which would afford Bill full view of the saloon. Having won some hands earlier and superstitious about changing seats, Charlie declined Bill's request. When Bill told Charlie that he didn't want to sit with his exposed back to the open bar and a rear doorway, Mann and Massie told the legendary gunfighter that he had no cause for concern.

Grumbling, Wild Bill took the lone empty seat at the table, his penchant for playing poker obviously outweighing his desire for self-preservation. In this, most researchers agree. But what occurred next is often a matter of conjecture.

Some sources claim that Wild Bill had played poker at this very table the night before. In one hand that night, Bill had made a large wager that a young miner known as Bill Sutherland had matched using a small bag of gold dust. When Wild Bill won the hand, the bag was taken to a scale at the end of the bar and weighed, where it was discovered it was light by as much as $18.

Often patient when payment was due, Wild Bill nonetheless demanded immediate settlement from the miner. Sutherland went out to his camp, gathered enough gold dust to settle his debt, then returned and gave it to Wild Bill. Suspecting the payment had busted Sutherland, Bill offered him enough loose change to buy breakfast. Sutherland declined the generous offer.

The next afternoon, after Wild Bill had been playing poker with Mann, Massie, and Rich for about three hours, Sutherland walked through the doors of the No. 10 Saloon. In short order his real name would be discovered to be John or Jack McCall. But Wild Bill apparently recognized the miner from the previous night's action and adjudged him no threat.

As betting between Wild Bill and Massie heated up, McCall gradually moved toward the rear door of the saloon and into the blind spot of arguably the most famous person in Deadwood. As Wild Bill lost a poker hand to Massie, commenting, "the old duffer, he broke me on that hand," McCall quickly walked up behind him, pulled a pistol from beneath his clothes, and fired one deadly shot into the back of Wild Bill's head, while shouting, "Damn you, take that!" The bullet exited Wild Bill's face just below his right eye, then lodged in the wrist of Captain Massie, who had been seated directly across the table from Wild Bill. As Bill fell from his stool and to the barroom floor, never to speak again, he spilled pairs of black aces and eights, forever after known as "The Dead Man's Hand."

Wild Bill Hickok
Courtesy City of Deadwood Archives

Those in the saloon were dumbstruck, even with an armed McCall waving his pistol around the room and screaming, "Come on ye sons a bitches." He cocked the hammer again and pulled the trigger, only to have the gun misfire. Nearly everyone fled from the armed madman. Only Mann stayed behind to assist Wild Bill, dead on the floor, unmoving.

It must have become quite clear to Mann as the gun smoke dissipated in his saloon that afternoon that a legend of the frontier had died that day. Along with the president of the United States, Sitting Bull, Buffalo Bill Cody, and Col. George Armstrong Custer (who had been killed just six weeks earlier at the Battle of the Little Bighorn), Wild Bill Hickok was among the nation's best-known individuals. Bolstered by popular dime-store novels and magazine features, Wild Bill's exploits, real and imagined, had brought him a level of fame he neither sought nor with which he was ever comfortable.

"In many ways he was the most remarkable of the old-time plainsmen," wrote Springfield, Missouri, newspaperman Alanson M. Haswell. "He had served in the Springfield region as a Union scout during the Civil War. He must be some thirty-five years of age, a magnificent specimen of manhood, tall and straight as an arrow, with his light brown hair hanging down to his shoulders under his broad-brimmed hat. He was a figure to attract attention anywhere.

"Like others of his profession, he had led a rather dissipated life and was beginning to show the marks thereof. But he was still in the prime of his strength and was one of the most kind-hearted and jovial men I have ever met. No one would have imagined that this genial man could have killed so long a list of men, but the circumstances of his life were such that time and again nothing saved his life but his marvelous quick use of a revolver. From all I have heard, there was never a case where it was not a justifiable shooting."

Often described as the "Prince of Pistoleers," Wild Bill had served as deputy U.S. marshal in Fort Hays, Kansas; sheriff of Ellis County at Hays; city marshal of Abilene, Kansas; and briefly a government scout and Wild West Show performer. Handsome, elegant in his speech, and prone to dress more like an eastern dandy than a frontier gunfighter, Wild Bill's reputation had preceded him to Deadwood, much as it had throughout the West for the decade past.

And now he was dead.

Researchers of Hickok's life claim he knew his time on the trail was coming to an end. In late August, after Wild Bill's burial, the *Cheyenne Daily Leader* published the following article under the headline, WILD BILL'S PRESENTIMENT.

"A week before Wild Bill's death he was heard to remark to a friend, I feel that my days are numbered; my days are sinking fast; I know I shall be killed here, something tells me I shall never leave these hills alive; somebody is going to kill me. But I don't know who it is or why he is going to do it. I have killed many men in my day, but I never killed a man yet but what it was kill or get killed with me . . ."

As author and historian Joseph G. Rosa notes in his definitive account of Hickok's life, *Wild Bill Hickok: The Man & His Myth*, the prophecy published after Hickok's death could easily be discounted. Perhaps, more credible it seems, is a letter Wild Bill wrote to his new wife the day before he was gunned down: "Agnes Darling, if such should be we never meet again, while firing my last shot, I will gently breathe the name of my wife—Agnes—and with wishes even for my enemies I will make the plunge and try to swim to the other shore. J. B. Hickok, Wild Bill."

In the course of human history, many a man of dubious character and questionable accomplishment has sought to enhance his own repu-tation, and indeed ensure his immortality, by assassinating someone who was revered, well known, and well liked. Jack McCall was one such individual, lacking in personal ambition, unaccustomed to success, and by all measures a no-account drifter of absolutely no distinction.

After firing the shot that killed Hickok, and then threatening all oth-ers within sight with a gun that wouldn't work, McCall fled through the saloon's rear doorway, ran down an alleyway, and then attempted to gain some ground by stealing a horse that was tied off nearby. However, much to McCall's dismay, when he leaped into the saddle, he discovered its owner had loosened the cinch. The saddle slid sideways and McCall fell to the ground. Panicked and fearing the same frontier justice he had just administered, the assassin likely headed west up the alley, then veered onto Main Street in his attempted escape.

While historians have long debated McCall's reasons for shooting Wild Bill, the purported path of his attempted escape, and the place of his eventual capture, it is clear that he was quickly recognized by townspeople and taken into custody. McCall cowered as he was led down Main Street, and a heavily armed and growing crowd called for his immediate hanging. Strong ropes materialized as he was led to one of the few remaining pine trees on Main Street.

McCall certainly would have been guest of honor at the necktie party were it not for one of the strangest coincidental occurrences ever to be chronicled in the Wild West. W. L. Kuykendall happened to be coming up Deadwood Gulch just as the townspeople, outraged at the cowardly manner in which McCall had killed Wild Bill, were preparing to hang him. According to Kuykendall's account, he witnessed "a large party of men in the twilight down the street, and going to them, it was found they had gathered to swing McCall to a pine limb, one of them having a rope for that purpose. The hanging, however, was suddenly abandoned and indefinitely postponed, when a Mexican came galloping up the street with the head of an Indian dangling from his side."

The Mexican horseman had brought the Indian's head to Deadwood to collect a $50 bounty offered by local businessmen in the wake of Custer's defeat a few weeks earlier in Montana. Of course, the bounty was for the scalp of any dead Indian—man, woman, or child—and not for the entire head, but apparently the bounty hunter wanted no question that the Indian was indeed dead.

The strange event turned the crowd's immediate attention away from McCall, and he was secured in a cabin while his fate was determined. That night, city leaders elected Judge Kuykendall to serve as judge for McCall's trial. Because Deadwood didn't officially yet exist and was at that time, in fact, part of the Great Sioux Reservation, no city, state, or federal court could convene in an attempt to ascertain McCall's guilt or innocence. So it was decided that the next morning a hastily called miner's court would select a jury, conduct the trial, and determine what punishment, if any, should be levied.

At 9:30 a.m. on August 3, court convened and it was determined that Bill Sutherland was indeed John McCall, and that prior to coming to the Black Hills, he had commonly been known as Jack McCall. As the jury was being selected through the remainder of the morning at the Deadwood Theater, a small, sad group of locals filed by Wild Bill's open coffin at Charlie Utter's camp to take one last look at the legendary lawman, soldier, scout, and spy. One observer later wrote, "I have seen many dead men on the field of battle, and in civil life, but Wild Bill was the prettiest corpse I have ever seen. His long mustache was attractive, even in death, and his long tapering fingers looked like marble."

At 2:00 p.m., the trial of Jack McCall, perhaps the first conducted in Deadwood, began. An hour later, as testimony continued downtown, Wild Bill Hickok was laid to rest in the town's new Mount Moriah Cemetery. Back at the theater, McCall had entered a plea of not guilty and testified succinctly that he had killed Wild Bill because Hickok had murdered his brother in Kansas. Two of the three men, believed to be Carl Mann and Captain Massie, with whom Wild Bill had been playing cards, gave eyewitness testimony.

Others testified to the appearance before the shooting of both the victim and his alleged killer. As testimony continued later than expected and, noting the theater would be needed for a performance that night, Judge Kuykendall elected to move the entire proceeding to the No. 10 Saloon, where the jury could deliberate, bring back its expected verdict of guilty, and the hanging could begin. However, after little more than an hour's deliberation, the jury returned with a verdict just the opposite of what had been anticipated.

Wild Bill's admirers were appalled. Some claimed they'd kill McCall at the slightest provocation. Others argued that they should hang him anyway, regardless of the verdict. Still others, prosecutor Col. George May and soon-to-be-sheriff Seth Bullock among them, suggested the jurors had been the same individuals who had paid McCall to kill Hickok, fearing the veteran lawman would soon be engaged to clean up Deadwood. Colonel May was so incensed that, when a fearful McCall rode away the next day, May followed him all the way to Laramie, Wyoming, where he listened as McCall publicly boasted of killing Wild Bill and getting away with it. May moved quickly, obtained a bench warrant, and succeeded in having McCall rearrested by deputy U.S. marshals on August 29. During a hearing McCall was remanded to the territorial capital at Yankton on a charge of murder.

On October 18 McCall was formally indicted at the U.S. District Courthouse in Yankton, where he again pleaded "not guilty." He was returned to his cell to await trial, but on November 9 he and his cellmate, Jerry McCarty, overpowered their jailer and attempted escape. Subdued by other lawman, and fearing his attempt to flee would prejudice his upcoming murder trial, McCall tried to turn state's evidence by claiming he had been hired to kill Wild Bill. But nothing came of the last-ditch effort and McCall's trial began December 1, in Yankton.

Evidence presented during the six-day trial was overwhelming, leading jurors to no other conclusion than that McCall had committed the cold-blooded assassination of Wild Bill Hickok. On the evening of December 6, McCall was found guilty and sentencing was set for January 3, 1877.

Although several attempts were made by McCall's defense attorneys to have the sentence commuted (they claimed variously that Wild Bill was a known gunman with violent tendencies, that McCall acted in self-defense, and that he killed Wild Bill to avenge his brother's death), the court learned that McCall had no brother and discounted his other claims. On January 3 Chief Justice P. C. Shannon pronounced sentence as follows: "[Y]ou John McCall, alias Jack McCall, be remanded hence to the place whence you came, that you be imprisoned until Thursday the first day of March, A.D., 1877, upon which day you shall be thence conducted to the place of execution, where, between the hours of 9 o'clock in the forenoon and two o'clock in the afternoon of the said day, you shall be hanged by the neck until you shall be dead. And may the Lord have mercy upon your soul."

On the morning of March 1, as a drizzling rain fell on the capital of Dakota Territory, Jack McCall, clutching a crucifix given him by an attending clergyman, was led to a small platform eight feet from the ground. A marshal placed a rope around McCall's neck. At 10:15 the trapdoor holding McCall's life gave way and he dropped into eternity, achieving the immortality he had apparently sought in killing one of the legends of the plains. His body was cut down, placed in a simple wooden casket with the noose still around his neck, and buried in an unmarked grave in the local Catholic cemetery.

Thomas Egan

Death of an Innocent

Thomas Egan left his Irish homeland in 1855 and traveled four thousand miles to find a new life in a promising land called America. What he found instead was a twisted tragedy, a leading role in one of Dakota Territory's first legal executions, and his death at the end of a hangman's noose for a crime he didn't commit.

Arriving in Philadelphia on June 16, 1855, Thomas and his sister, Maria, immediately headed west. Working their way to Madison, Wisconsin, the two surveyed a scene of farmlands flowing to the horizon. Rich river bottoms and green and rolling hillsides must have reminded Thomas and his sister of their native land. Thomas found work in a lead mine through an Irish relative and he met a widow and mother named Mary Hayden Lyons, who was still working the farm she and her now-deceased husband had started. Mary's daughter, Catherine, was nearing six years of age when Thomas Egan and her mother wed at a church in Madison in 1866.

As they settled into their new life and Thomas warmed to his new step-daughter, he and his wife looked farther west where new lands were being opened to adventurous homesteaders. They eventually were caught up in the parade to the prairie. With two new sons, Sylvester and John, they moved to north central Iowa and helped relatives work their farm for three years. A third son, Tommy, was born in Iowa. But Thomas longed for his own farm.

The quiet and often introverted Thomas led an oxcart and his family to Sioux Falls. Young Catherine stayed with relatives in Iowa with the understanding that she would join the family once they had settled their homestead. The Egans found a 160-acre plot twenty miles northwest of

Egan family

Photo courtesy of C. John Egan Jr.

Sioux Falls on Grand Meadow Township farmland. Before they left the land office in Sioux Falls, as some thirty-four thousand immigrants did before statehood in 1889, they also owned a separate timber claim. It was a dream come true for Thomas.

The Egans were invigorated by their initial success and the prospect of building a successful farm for themselves. As their new property came into view, with tall cottonwoods and a small, gurgling brook, all of their earlier fears faded away. Within a month Thomas had built a two-room shanty and crafted beds, stools, and a table to furnish the two rooms. A shallow cellar was dug beneath the house to allow for the storage of kindling and foodstuffs. A cast-iron stove in the main room was fired with dried oxen droppings, grasses, or wood scraps.

As Thomas began planting crops, Mary sought housework and sewing to supplement the family income. While they waited for the autumn harvest, Thomas and his three sons dug a well and built stable sheds to protect livestock from harsh winter weather.

Two years after staking claim to their private paradise, they welcomed daughter Catherine back into the fold. The Egans endured the harsh winter of 1877–78 huddled in their simple shanty. With two adults, a distant teenage daughter, and three young boys, the confinement caused by howling winds and frequent snowstorms led to quarrels. Later, memories of those confrontations would take on monumental proportions and even lead Thomas and Mary to discuss their serious differences with divorce attorneys.

While Thomas and Mary grew apart, Catherine and neighbor James Van Horn were warming to each other. Following another season on the farm, Thomas's stepdaughter married Van Horn on November 23, 1879, and moved to his home. But Thomas resented William and James Van Horn, a resentment fueled by a dispute over the timber claim that Thomas held. He felt the Van Horns had their own plans for the claim. The disharmony led Catherine to visit her mother and stepfather only rarely, even though they lived on two neighboring farmsteads.

The crops in 1880 were outstanding for Thomas. After the harvest he prepared for another long winter when ample stocks of hay and firewood would be needed. This meant a two-day trip to the timber claim, where they could cut and rake hay and collect firewood, before transporting it back to the homestead on racks pulled by oxen.

On September 12, 1880, Thomas and his two youngest sons set out. As he drove his oxen down a dusty trail, the proud Irish immigrant probably contemplated the challenges of the coming winter. At the top of his mind, too, may have been his continuing contentious relationship with Mary. On the way Thomas stopped at the farm of Charlie Wells. Thomas and Charlie often shared work and Charlie agreed to bring a team of horses and a mower to Thomas's timber claim. The group arrived at the claim that afternoon, fed and watered the oxen and horses, fixed a simple meal, laid out their bedrolls, and slept.

At first light they shook off the morning chill by going to work. The boys mowed, raked, and stacked hay while Thomas and Charlie began digging a well. At the end of the day, the group wove its way back to Charlie's farm, where they slept. The next morning, Charlie and young John returned to the timber claim as Thomas and Tommy turned their full load of hay toward home. Along the way Thomas picked up another of his few friends, John Ryan, who would accompany the Egans to their plot and help unload.

As Ryan pitched hay onto a pile midway between the house and the stables, he heard a shout from the boy that would signal a drastic change in all their lives. Racing to the house, Ryan discovered Thomas and Tommy peering into the darkened main room of their shanty. It was clear something was amiss. The trapdoor to the cellar was askew and even in the dim light they could see what appeared to be blood surrounding the opening. Tommy went into the cellar and there, in the small dank underground crypt, he discovered the bloodied body of the only mother he had ever known.

"Mary is dead," he yelled to Ryan from below. "Dead or killed?"

Ryan responded. "Killed," Thomas answered. They studied a scene of struggle. Mary's clothing was caked with blood and a trail led to the bedroom. Thomas asked Ryan to help him carry Mary's body from the cellar to the kitchen table. Ryan declined. After tending to his oxen, Thomas walked with Ryan to his nearby homestead, where they informed Mary Ryan of the tragic story and asked her to get another neighbor to tend to Mary Egan's corpse.

When he arrived back at his homestead, through sheer habit, Thomas went to his barn to tend to his pigs. A few minutes later, he left the barn and discovered neighbors James Van Horn, Elon Warren, and Frank VanDeMark waiting on his stoop. Warren held a gun in his hand.

"Egan, what is up?" Van Horn asked. "Oh, Mary is dead," Thomas responded in such a simple way that it would later be construed as indifference. "Egan, you know how she came into the cellar, and you might as well own it up," a stern VanDeMark said.

While Thomas tried to explain where he'd been the last two days, meaning he could not have been at his homestead to commit the crime, his three neighbors proved to be an inattentive audience. At about 11:00 a.m., the three men took Thomas into custody, loaded him into a buggy, and slowly rolled their way to Sioux Falls. There, Egan was taken into custody and led to a jail cell. Over the next twenty-two months, it would remain his only home.

Authorities quickly formed a coroner's jury that traveled to the Egan house, inspected the body, and explored the homestead. But it would be more than a year before Thomas would see the inside of a courtroom.

As months of confinement rolled by, Thomas became friends with his fellow inmates as well as his captor, Sheriff Joe Dickson. In hours of talk Thomas continued to proclaim his innocence, telling all who would listen that he had been as surprised as anyone to find his wife dead in their homestead shack. When several prisoners escaped from the jail that summer, Egan was not among them. The fact Thomas stayed when others fled did not go unnoticed by the local newspaper, nor by Sheriff

Dickson. When priests and attorneys suggested he must be leaving something out of his story, Thomas would simply repeat his original denial: "I did not do it."

On November 25, 1881, examination of prospective jurors began in the Fourth Judicial District Court of Dakota Territory. Prosecutors and defense lawyers—Egan was represented by C. H. Winsor (the same lawyer his wife, Mary, had consulted about a divorce) and L. S. Swezey—grilled jurors on their beliefs, their feelings about the death penalty, and whether they had already formed a judgment about Egan's guilt or innocence. When Mary Egan's death was clearly one of the most popular topics in town, the defense requested a change of venue. It was quickly denied. Any potential juror with qualms about the death penalty was summarily excused. At the conclusion of jury selection, twelve men were chosen, including a lawyer, a carpenter, a harness maker, homesteaders, and farmworkers.

Egan was summoned to the courtroom, the indictment was read, and the prosecution began its case by calling the first of more than three dozen witnesses. Minnehaha County justice of the peace R. S. Hawkins described the cellar in which Mary was discovered and the condition of her body. He noted that her neck was marked, her head was matted with blood and dirt, and one arm was severely bruised.

Dr. Allen testified to the gruesome scene and the suspected cause of death. "I found evidence of violence, marks in the region of the head," he stated. The doctor said he observed "ragged, lacerated wounds" to Mary's head and attributed her death to either the obvious head wounds or by strangulation with a halter rope found at the scene.

Others who had visited the murder scene testified that, in some places, the blood was still moist, and that bloody clothes, some belonging to Thomas, had been found. The defense did not suggest that the blood on Thomas's clothes was the result of his finding the body, nor did they ask doctors and lawmen how long blood would remain moist following such a violent murder.

Thomas's arch nemesis, William Van Horn, testified, saying a few days after the murder he had visited the Egan homestead and discovered "a hardwood picket-pin 16 steps south of the house in the trees with blood on it and hair also. In a bunch of weeds." Incredibly, he then produced the picket-pin, which he had had in his possession for nearly fifteen months. When the defense objected on the grounds that no foundation had been laid for the evidence and that there was nothing to tie the defendant to the picket-pin, the objection was overruled.

Van Horn went on to describe his strained relationship with Thomas, testified that Thomas had told him he had never gotten along with his wife since marriage, and admitted that since Thomas had been jailed, he had contested the Egans' timber claim in an attempt to take possession of it.

Then a parade of family members took the stand. First, Thomas's stepdaughter, Catherine, said she had not seen her mother in the three weeks before her death. Eldest son Sylvester took the stand and claimed he was fourteen years old (he actually had turned thirteen two weeks before). Following the prosecution's script, Sylvester described the confrontational nature of the Egan household. His most damaging testimony came when he was asked about his father's treatment of his mother. The defense objected, but Judge Jefferson P. Kidder overruled. "He used to pound her, and abuse her, and call her all sorts of names," Sylvester said. He later added, "In June he struck her three times and knocked her down. I pulled him off and told him that was enough."

The district attorney, smelling the kill, asked how Thomas had responded to the son's intervention. "He called her all sorts of names—damned bitch and whore, and lying rip . . . Mother said she was not. He picked up a knife and said if she said another word, he would cut her throat." The suspense in the courtroom was palpable. In the only words Thomas Egan spoke at trial, he told one of his attorneys, "Mr. Swezey, I don't want to hear that boy talk that way." He was not overruled.

Others testified that they had witnessed Thomas's wrath toward his wife. In his second appearance on the stand, James Van Horn confirmed Thomas's mistreatment of Mary, recalling "abusive language." He noted that when he heard Mary was dead, he immediately assumed Thomas had killed her. The defense objected to the testimony and the prosecutor agreed that Van Horn's remark should be stricken from the record, but the damage already had been done.

Van Horn and two neighbors testified that Thomas told them he had another woman waiting for him when he was "rid of this one." And finally, after a parade of prosecution witnesses, the district attorney chose Thomas's youngest sons, John and Tommy, to complete their case. Neither boy's testimony was favorable for their father.

After thirty-nine witnesses had offered no direct, physical, or corroborating evidence whatsoever that tied Thomas Egan to the murder of his wife, the prosecution rested its case. Then, without pause or deliberation, one of Thomas's attorneys proffered the most astonishing statement of the trial. Said defense attorney Swezey, "We have no testimony to put in."

With instructions rendered by Judge Kidder, the first jury to hear a murder case conducted by Dakota Territory rather than the federal government began its deliberations. The time spent deliberating was never recorded, but with no defense arguments to cloud their discussions or even remotely suggest the innocence of the accused, they were assuredly short. When the guilty verdict was read, it likely surprised no one, save Thomas Egan.

As dirty snows melted on the plains of Dakota Territory in the spring of 1882, someone added a further humiliation to Thomas's plight when they burned to the ground all of the buildings on the Egan homestead. In May the Territorial Supreme Court upheld the findings of the lower court, and later that month, Minnehaha County set execution for July 13.

When Thomas was resentenced, the judge asked if he knew of any reason why he should not be sentenced to death. The homesteader, who had spoken but one sentence in the course of his trial, angrily replied, "Judge, I have nothing against anybody in the court, nor anybody around this country except the Van Horns. They betrayed me, and may the curse of God rest upon them." After the judge proclaimed sentence, Thomas said, "All right sir, I can stand it. The law may not reach the Van Horns, but the curse of God will, and all those who betrayed me."

Twenty months had passed since his wife's death and his hard landing in jail. Thomas had now spent twenty-five of his forty-five years of life in America. And now he was going to die.

Three days before the scheduled execution, workmen began building a heavy gallows adjacent to the Minnehaha County Jail. On the morning of his execution, Thomas was awakened at 5:00 a.m. by a Father Maher and received communion. A barber shaved him and trimmed his black mustache, beard, and hair. Thomas had a breakfast of beef steak, eggs, potatoes, coffee, bread and butter, and cake. At 9:05 he asked if it was time to go outside. Five minutes later, dressed in a clean white shirt and black suit, shoes, and tie, he listened as his death sentence was read. At 9:30 the sheriff tied his arms behind him and told Thomas it was time.

A hush fell over the crowd surrounding the gallows as Thomas was led outside. None could have forecast what brutality awaited the condemned. As C. John Egan Jr. would later so ably write, "This was a day the recollection of which demonstrates the ability of historical truth to captivate, to tell a story more fascinating than any in fiction."

When he had reached the top of the scaffold, Thomas was asked if he wished to say anything. In a low voice, he said, "No." A hood was placed over his head, a noose around his neck. Only the chanting of the priest's prayer could be heard. According to those in attendance, the release of the trapdoor sounded like the crack of gunfire. "Egan dropped like a large sack of seed corn," C. John Egan Jr. wrote in *Drop Him Till He Dies*. "When the rope reached full length, Egan's body snapped viciously. Then, like a huge broken doll, he tumbled the remaining distance to the ground. Astonishingly, the rope had broken."

Spectators let loose an audible gasp, as Thomas's hooded body hit the ground. Newspapers would later describe the gruesome scene. "[There is] a gurgling sound. He is strangling. His neck is not broken." The *St. Paul Pioneer Press* added that half a dozen men came forward to assist Sheriff Dickson in returning a groaning Thomas to the platform, the broken rope still dangling from his neck. Amid cries from prisoners held inside the jail, claiming that a condemned man could be hanged but once, the sheriff and his men began making adjustments to the new rope, noose, and hood that covered Thomas's head. As they did so, the trapdoor was inadvertently released and the half-dead Thomas plunged once again some seven feet to the ground.

For a third time, authorities escorted Thomas to the platform and when the trapdoor once again was released, a successful snap signaled the end of this strange story of frontier justice.

The dust was brushed off Thomas's suit. His remains were placed in a simple casket, destined for burial in an unmarked grave. The hideous nature of Thomas's execution, compounded by the weakness of the defense he had been provided at trial, was ignored as the territory raced toward statehood in 1889. The sad realities of Thomas Egan's demise wouldn't be known for forty-five years after his death. On June 3, 1927, as a widowed sixty-five-year-old Catherine Van Horn lay dying in a Seattle hospital room, she sought to make peace with her soul and the higher power that would soon judge her. Catherine called to her bedside Dr. W. C. Woodward and others.

"Back in South Dakota, in the early '80s, I killed my mother," Catherine said. "I did not live far from my mother. One day when my stepfather and the kids were away from home, I went to my mother's. We quarreled. I hit her over the head with a picket-pin. She fell to the floor. I hit her again and again. Then I realized she was dead. I was terribly frightened, so I opened the trapdoor of the cellar, shoved her through the hole, carefully closed the door, and fled.

"After I got outside, I noticed the picket-pin was still in my hand. I threw it away. I looked cautiously around. No one was in sight. No one would ever know what I had done. Then I turned and ran as fast as I could. No one ever suspected me. My stepfather, Thomas Egan, was hung for the crime. He died avowing his innocence."

Thus, the true story of the lonely life and wrongful death of Thomas Egan, the first man to be legally hanged by Dakota Territory officials, came to pass. He had come to the United States to pursue a dream. Instead he had discovered a nightmare that led to his death at age forty-seven in the first of only fifteen state-sanctioned executions in the last 125 years. Following Egan's execution, it took another forty-five years to exonerate him—to determine that the horrific story of his wife's death, his outlandish trial, and his horrendous execution were truly not of his own making.

Crow Dog
Killing Spotted Tail

On a hot August day in 1881, Rosebud police captain Crow Dog stopped his wagon, grabbed his gun, and, squinting against the incessant sun, watched closely as his vaunted rival—Spotted Tail—approached on horseback. As the dust from Spotted Tail's pony came closer, Crow Dog's hand tightened on his pistol grip. Placing the wagon between himself and his adversary, Crow Dog watched as Spotted Tail's horse slowed and then stopped, just fifteen feet away. Sensing motion, Crow Dog leveled his gun, pulled back on the trigger, and sent an explosion rippling across the parched prairie.

Spotted Tail fell from his mount, never to rise again.

With a lone bullet Crow Dog had changed a tribe. As the blast from Crow Dog's handgun echoed through the creek-carved coulees, it sent reverberations that would resonate for longer than his lifetime, from the grasslands of the Great Plains to the hallowed halls of the U.S. Supreme Court.

And, in the end, an aging Crow Dog would walk free and return to the people who had disowned him—and some who disavow him still.

As members of the Brule band of the Lakota, Crow Dog and Spotted Tail had been raised together. They had vied for the same honors, sought the same affections, and strove to each help direct the actions of their people during a time when the world all around them was changing. The buffalo herds had been replaced by bluecoats, and the Plains Indians were largely relegated to living a life of subsistence on government reservations. Crow Dog and Spotted Tail were contemporaries but also were fiercely competitive with one another.

Known as Kan-gi-shun-ka to his brethren, Crow Dog disliked the way the fifty-five-year-old Spotted Tail ruled the Brule bands and was one of his most frequent and vocal critics. In response Spotted Tail had twice been involved in having Crow Dog discharged from the tribal police force. In December 1880 Crow Dog's political differences had led him to argue for Spotted Tail's removal as chief, saying he was incompetent to govern.

They had gathered in council on the Rosebud on August 5, 1881, ostensibly to discuss the government's desire to have the Lakota nation cede back a strip of land along the Niobrara River to the Poncas. Spotted Tail favored the request while Crow Dog and his followers were strongly opposed. Harsh words were uttered. Allies of both men quietly told Crow Dog and Spotted Tail that the other wished him irreparable harm. When the council retired, Crow Dog set out for his camp with his wife of two decades—Pretty Camp—in his horse-pulled wagon. At his feet rattled an old pistol and a box with ten cartridges. Galloping in Crow Dog's tracks was Spotted Tail, wearing a striped calico shirt and hat and wrapped in a blue blanket.

When Crow Dog stopped his wagon to fix a loose board, he saw Spotted Tail trotting toward him. His heart beating violently in his chest, Crow Dog got down from the wagon, grabbed his gun, and, as Spotted Tail approached, thumbed it to half cock. Staring into each other's face, not a word was spoken between the two men. When he thought Spotted Tail was reaching for his gun, Crow Dog quickly aimed and fired. The bullet penetrated Spotted Tail's left side, exited his right, and killed him almost instantly.

"Had gone to horses to unwind a line when a person approached on horseback, at a gallop, from direction of council lodge, whom I recognized as Spotted Tail," Crow Dog would later testify, according to the *Black Hills Daily Times*. He "checked his horse into a walk—as he approached he seemed to be searching for weapon in the vicinity of his hip; my wife said something which I did not understand. Saw from facial

Crow Dog
Photo courtesy of the Adams Museum

expression of Spotted Tail that trouble was on hand; deceased halted— drew his pistol—leveled it at me when I fired and killed him; run around wagon and was putting in another cartridge—thinking I had missed him."

Crow Dog said he was afraid of Spotted Tail and had taken his adversary's purported threats to heart. "I meant what I said," Crow Dog told the court at his murder trial seven months after the shooting. "It had come to my ears that the deceased entertained very hostile feelings towards me, and, knowing the man, I knew what that meant . . . (I) resolved not to be shot if I could avoid it."

When the smoke had cleared and Spotted Tail lay dead on the ground, Crow Dog fled to his camp on the White River while mourn- ers, hearing of the shooting, carried the remains to a nearby home. News of the shooting quickly spread throughout the reservation, then on to the nearest major cities of St. Paul and Chicago. When Gen. John Cook, the agent at Rosebud, read about the killing in the *St. Paul Pioneer Press*, he feared further bloodshed and caught the first train back to his assigned post.

Three days after Spotted Tail died, General Cook told the *Pioneer Press* that "Spotted Tail was one of the best Indians his long experience had ever brought him in contact with" and described the departed as "faithful, honorable and influential."

In the wake of the shooting, newspapers speculated about the rea- sons for Spotted Tail's death and offered their own theories as to what would occur next. The *Black Hills Daily Times* surmised that Crow Dog had followed his unarmed victim knowing Spotted Tail had left his weapon at home. "Crow Dog followed him, and taking advantage of his defenseless condition shot him down," the *Times* reported a week after the incident. "Crow Dog had better make his will. Spotted Tail Jr., a tall, brave, active young man, will as surely kill him on sight as he would destroy a venomous snake, and there will be few to say him nay."

The same day, newspaper reports heralded the fallen Brule leader and offered reflections from soldiers who had known him. "Majors

Gordon of the Second, and Ball of the Seventh cavalry both remembered Spotted Tail well, and describe him as a man of five feet nine inches in height, well proportioned, light copper-colored in complexion, and with a general air of dignity and intelligence," the *Times* stated. "They first saw him at Fort Laramie in 1866, he having come thither on an errand so sad that it has visibly affected his after life.

"He brought there the body of his favorite daughter for burial, and officers of the post and other white residents of the vicinity took part in the obsequies. Spotted Tail killed a number of ponies at the funeral and nailed the skulls on the posts supporting the coffin. There the skulls still remain, and every year the commanding officers at Laramie see to it that the coffin is decorated with flowers and streamers."

Fifteen days after the violent confrontation, General Cook arrested Crow Dog and Black Crow, described as an accomplice, and sent them to Fort Niobrara for confinement until they could be turned over to the U.S. marshal for trial. Newspaper reports speculated that the murder was a conspiracy to remove Spotted Tail from power and allow Black Crow to be named chief. "The prompt arrest of the murderers broke up the conspiracy. All is quiet at the agency," the *Times* stated.

On St. Patrick's Day 1882, when jury selection began in the Crow Dog murder trial, prospective jurors were questioned on whether they would value the testimony of witnesses regardless of their race. "I could not," answered one white potential juror. "The testimony of one white man would go further with me than that of one hundred Indians."

When Crow Dog was finally arraigned in territorial court in Deadwood, attorney A. J. Plowman was assigned as defense counsel. In its opening statement the prosecution noted that Spotted Tail had been proclaimed chief of the Brule tribe of the Sioux by the famed Indian fighter Gen. George Crook in 1876. Spotted Tail had "devoted himself and his utmost energy to an observance of all the treaty stipulations to be observed by his people." His efforts were countered by warlike elements of the tribe, and those agitators were led in spirit by the defendant, Crow

Dog, prosecutors contended. Furthermore, after years of bad words and at the insistence of Spotted Tail, Crow Dog had been dismissed as chief of police just a month before he gunned down Spotted Tail.

A succession of witnesses followed, including General Cook, the Rosebud agent, and Spotted Tail's allies, Chasing Hawk, Thigh, Stinking Foot, and High Bear. The victim's sons, Windy Horse and Spotted Tail Jr., testified, the latter about first seeing his dead father and the funeral services conducted the following day by the agency missionary, a Father Cleveland. Spotted Tail's widow, Hill's Mother, said her husband had carried no weapon to the council on the day of his death and thus was unarmed when he was killed.

When the prosecution rested, defense attorney Plowman called Crow Dog's wife to the stand. Prosecutors were able to exclude all of her testimony when the court ruled that the couple was not legally wedded, despite the fact they had been together for twenty-one years and that the federal government recognized Pretty Camp as Crow Dog's wife on government rolls.

Seven months after he had shot Spotted Tail, Crow Dog took the stand in his own defense and testified that he had been acting in self-defense. With the aid of an interpreter, Crow Dog said that Spotted Tail had threatened and pursued him, had reached for his weapon in a menacing manner, and had created a situation that led to his own death.

Plowman reserved his most convincing arguments for closing, contending that Crow Dog's actions were irrelevant because the court had no jurisdiction in the case.

"It is not the power of congress to punish such offenses as have arisen in this case," Plowman argued. "In short, is there any law of congress which makes the acts alleged in this indictment a crime, what is the punishment and what court has jurisdiction? We claim that no such offense is known to the laws of the United States, no punishment has been provided, and that this court has no jurisdiction of the person of the defendant or of the crime alleged."

Plowman continued by saying that the matter of Spotted Tail's death had already been handled by tribal council and that the defendant had met with the victim's family, whom he had compensated in the traditional manner of the tribe with money, sugar, blankets, and ponies. To cap his closing, the defense counsel made an emotional appeal.

"Put away your prejudices and forget the race of this defendant," said Plowman, who had proffered Crow Dog's appeal without compensation and had borne much of the defendant's incidental expenses of the trial. "They are not worthy of lodgment in your human breasts—brush them away, sweep them aside and give us at your hands a verdict commensurate with the evidence and the law as the court shall give it to you."

After the jury was charged, deliberations began at 4:45 p.m. and went all night. At 9:15 a.m., March 25, 1882, the jury returned to the courtroom and announced that Crow Dog had been found "guilty of murder as charged in the first count of the indictment." Plowman made an immediate motion for a new trial.

Within hours of the guilty verdict, the *Times* reported that the jury's decision was "the greatest surprise to everybody that could well be imagined . . . The evidence as adduced during the trial has been closely analyzed by everybody and the unanimous opinion of all is that the defendant should have been acquitted."

When he was sentenced to death four days later, the same newspaper remarked about a decided change in Crow Dog's behavior, as well as that of his supporters. "Yesterday, when sentence of death was being passed by the court upon Crow Dog, that brute laughed and seemed highly pleased. Where were the sentimentalists who were with him during the trial? They had all deserted him—none were in the courtroom."

Four months later, with Crow Dog still confined to a jail cell, townspeople speculated as to the brave's eventual fate. Although some thought he would be hanged, others did not "believe our government will ever harm a hair of his head for his present offense." On April 4, 1882, the *Times* noted that Crow Dog had received a respite until at least

June 4. When the Territorial Supreme Court affirmed the lower court's findings and death sentence later that year, editorials called for a pardon of Crow Dog and petitions were started.

Following his trial, conviction, and sentencing, Crow Dog was granted remarkable liberties while in jail. Weeks before his scheduled execution, Crow Dog requested permission to visit his home on the Rosebud, say farewell to his wife and two young boys, and straighten his affairs. Astonishingly, his request was granted and he set out under escort of a deputy marshal.

While the deputy remained at the agency, Crow Dog visited his home with the promise he would return the next day. When he had not appeared by the appointed time, the deputy dispatched Indian police to apprehend him. Arriving at Crow Dog's humble home, police did not find him. Pretty Camp told them that Crow Dog had preferred to ride back to prison alone and would reach there on the agreed-upon day. While the deputy and tribal police scurried to find the fugitive, the next day a telegram arrived from Rapid City informing them that Crow Dog had reported there on his way back to jail in Deadwood.

As 1894 dawned, just fourteen days before his scheduled execution and after more than two years of confinement and legal wrangling, the U.S. Supreme Court set aside the Crow Dog verdict, agreeing with Plowman's contention that a state or territorial court had no jurisdiction on an Indian reservation, setting a precedent for Indians committing a crime on a reservation who were subsequently tried by state or territorial courts. A smiling Crow Dog was immediately released from jail.

"The old veteran walked forth a free man, after a confinement of more than two years," the gleeful *Times* reported. "He came downtown alone, shaking hands with every man he had ever seen before, saying that his heart was good, and that the white men were 'washta.' Frank Zipp presented him with a pair of German socks and a pair of Arctic overshoes, and [now] Judge Plowman rigged him out with a heavy woolen shirt, coat and ulster."

Crow Dog returned to his Brule band and led a quiet life still filled with heartache for the long ago and the enemies his actions had created. Nearly six years after his release from confinement, in the midst of the Ghost Dance craze, and just two days after Sitting Bull was killed by tribal police officers, Crow Dog wrote his old friend Judge Plowman and described his fate.

"My Friend," Crow Dog began his December 17, 1890, correspondence from the Pine Ridge Reservation. "Today I have come into this agency from the Bad Lands, and I thought I would write you a short letter. The Rosebud people . . . have been using me badly, so I left there. So now I have no friends left. So I have come here with my band, and left behind me those who have mistreated me . . .

"Now I tell of what is wild. At all the agencies the soldiers have come. They have drove some of the Indians from place to place, and they have caused me to come here. And some white men at the Cheyenne river killed one of our young men, and we feel bad about it. It almost kills me, and I feel like a living ghost. But for all that I try to keep up a good heart. You are my friend and the Indian's friend, and I would like you to help and recognize us. Write and tell me what you think. Your friend, Crow Dog."

Two weeks later, Lakota blood seeped into the snows of the new state of South Dakota. Crow Dog remained one of the last holdouts following the massacre of Chief Big Foot and his followers at Wounded Knee on December 29, 1890. The proud Lakota leader, who had carried out his own death sentence on Chief Spotted Tail, survived his own sentence of death from a white man's court, and changed U.S. law for all time, finished his remaining years in quiet obscurity on the Rosebud Reservation.

Lee "Curly" Grimes
Everyone Approved of His Demise

Scrambling for freedom on the second day of February 1880, with two of the baddest bounty hunters in the Black Hills following his trail, Lee "Curly" Grimes was a man without sanctuary. Although a blizzard had blanketed the plains of western South Dakota, the gunman Curly wasn't savoring a warm jail cell or a roaring fire. Instead, he was seeking a fast horse and a quiet escape. Behind him rode Detective William H. Llewellyn and D. Boone May, the latter known as a capable crime fighter who wasn't overly concerned with the intricacies of the judicial system.

Curly had been tied to the Doc Middleton Gang, a nasty bunch of stage robbers and rustlers who had been plaguing the dusty trails around Deadwood.

The previous summer, Curly and two associates had committed a series of stage robberies. After his two accomplices were captured, Curly joined a freighting outfit and attempted to hide amidst the bull-whackers and wagons as they wove their way down the Fort Pierre Road. But "road" was a misnomer for this winding trail between the Black Hills and the mighty Missouri. The route spanned coulees, ridges, and vast open grasslands where the summer sun could be brutally hot and a winter ground blizzard could freeze a cow standing still.

During the fall of 1879 and the winter of 1880, authorities were on the lookout for the acclaimed gunmen known as Curly. As far as they knew, Curly was a deadbeat desperado who liked to borrow livestock and gold. He was known to have driven off eighteen head of horses from the Rawhide Buttes area. It was only a matter of time before ungracious gold companies and frustrated stockmen took exception to the manner in which Curly was earning his living.

May had a reputation for bringing outlaws to justice. Some claimed his abilities with a gun were second only to those of Wild Bill Hickok. And when the "Prince of Pistoleers" was gunned down playing poker in a Deadwood saloon four years earlier, in the estimation of some, that left Boone May at the top of the heap. He was a favorite of Wells Fargo officials, who hired special messengers and men like May to guard their gold-laden stages as they were leaving the Black Hills.

Special messengers were expected to protect the shipments at any cost and to rid the region of outlaws whenever they crawled out from a cave or from under a rock. Wells Fargo & Co. and mining officials didn't particularly care how that was accomplished. Nor did the heavy-handed Boone May.

May was a rancher and fast-draw credited with the capture of many men, and the mysterious deaths of several others. On one widely reported occasion, while guarding a gold shipment, May shot the outlaw Frank Towle. After delivering his cargo, May learned that Towle had died and been buried near the scene of the shootout. Because of a $200 bounty on the man's head, May returned to the site, dug up Towle's grave, and literally cut off the dead man's head. He stuffed the cranium in a bag and carried it around to several county commission meetings hoping one would pay the bounty. When May couldn't prove that he had actually killed the highwayman, none did.

For his part Curly was regarded as a crafty criminal, an extraordinary gunman, and a confirmed killer. One newspaper reported that Doc Middleton had kicked Curly out of his mob "because the bandit deemed him too bad to belong to his gang of horse thieves and cutthroats." Old-timers claimed Curly had "perfected a system of 'rolling' the hammers of his guns with both hands and firing with tremendous rapidity and accuracy," wrote the *Black Hills Daily Times*. In another account from writer and historian Agnes Wright Spring, Curly was described as "a 'dead' shot and evidently had invented a system of his own which would shoot his guns more rapidly than a trigger would operate them."

Grimes had ridden his horse from Texas (where he was suspected of taking part in the robbery of $65,000 in gold coin from the Union Pacific Express) to Nebraska in the spring of 1877. While herding cattle for a ranch on the Niobrara River, he reportedly made off with fifteen head for himself. He also stopped by the Boon Creek Post Office on July 5, 1877, where he took $17 in postage stamps, one thousand rounds of ammunition, and a new suit of clothes belonging to the postmaster.

Knowing of the suspect's skill with a gun, Detective Llewellyn enlisted the aid of May, whose reputation was arguably as questionable as the outlaw they sought to capture. When they received word that Curly had signed on with Morris Appel's freight line, the two well-armed bounty hunters set out on horseback to find him. As the temperature dipped below freezing, Llewellyn and May caught up with Curly at the Morris ranch along the Fort Pierre Road, about thirty-five miles northeast of Deadwood. At gunpoint the men arrested Curly, handcuffed him, and put him on a horse. Then they turned west into a bitter breeze for the long, cold ride back to Fort Meade near Sturgis.

The three horseman rode straight into a blinding blizzard. After sunset the thermometer dipped to twenty degrees below zero. At one point Curly asked his captors if his iron handcuffs could be removed so that his hands would not freeze. Llewellyn and May later asserted that Curly promised he wouldn't try to escape, so May removed the manacles. For seven more hours they rode on through the subzero darkness of a blinding blizzard.

At one point, when his horse floundered in two feet of snow as it left the trail, the mounted lawmen quickly caught up and ordered the fleeing man to halt. Curly ignored the command and both bounty hunters opened fire. Mortally injured in the back with shotgun pellets and gunshots, the outlaw dropped from his saddle to the ground and was dead before the two officers reached him. They placed Curly's hat over his lifeless face and rode on.

The reaction to Curly's killing was vocal and initially unanimous in support. The *Black Hills Daily Times* reported, "While en route to this city, and within a couple of miles from Fort Meade, Curly attempted to escape, and the only way they could prevent such result was to fire upon him, which they did with good effect, riddling his body with buckshot and pistol bullets.

"This occurred about 11 o'clock Monday night, and they left the dead crook on the ground where he fell," the *Times* continued. "The transaction was reported at Fort Meade, and a squad of soldiers went out yesterday and buried him. The action of the detectives in the matter is approved by every one we have heard express themselves."

The next day, the *Times* echoed its earlier pronouncement when it noted that the people of Deadwood were now "under lasting obligations to Llewellyn and May. The life and deeds of this outlaw will most probably never be known in detail, but enough is known to convince us that his room in the world is better than his company."

A few days later, with no official confirmation that Curly had been killed, the newspaper questioned the accounts of the two law officers. However, in a humbled report the next day, February 8, 1880, the newspaper lambasted itself for ever questioning the integrity of Llewellyn and May. "It became the common belief that there was something wrong, and the said reporter shared in the said common belief," the *Times* admitted. "But the reporter was wrong, as well as the common belief; for the remains of Curly were lying exposed out upon the open prairie, within sixty feet of the Sidney stage road yesterday morning, just where he fell, with the snow drifting about and over them. Sheriff Moulton of Pennington County, who came up last evening, saw the remains lying as described."

In the ensuing days, as news of Curly's untimely and violent demise reached the backwoods and mining claims of the Black Hills, some voiced condemnation of the summary manner of his death. Others argued over whether his remains should be dug up and examined by the coroner. When that actually occurred a week after the shooting—and when the amount of damage done to Curly's body was discovered—warrants were issued for the arrest of Llewellyn and May.

The pair turned themselves into authorities and bail was set at $10,000 for each of the lawmen-turned-suspects. In short order men representing $500,000 in assets posted the necessary bonds and Llewellyn and May walked free, pending trial. May immediately went to work for his friend, author and journalist Ambrose Bierce, then general agent of the Black Hills Placer Mining Company in Rockerville. While guarding a shipment of gold on a rainy night in the spring of 1880, May would have an opportunity to use his gun again.

Transporting $30,000 in company funds in an open wagon between Deadwood and Rockerville, May and Bierce encountered highwaymen on the trail. The outlaws ordered the two agents to "Throw up your hands!" As Bierce brought the team to a halt and reached for his weapon, May took care of business.

"With the quickest movements that I had ever seen in anything but a cat," Bierce later wrote, "May had thrown himself backward across the back of the seat, face upward, and the muzzle of his rifle was within a yard of the fellow's breast." While under indictment for one murder, May pulled the trigger and ended yet another miserable man's life.

On August 23, 1880, six months after the shooting, Llewellyn and May were brought to trial for the death of Curly Grimes.

When the prosecution presented its case, attorneys for the territorial government claimed the seventeen buckshot and pistol-ball wounds found in Curly's back might indicate a bit of overkill. But a parade of defense witnesses attested to Curly's cruel manner, criminal behavior, and unsavory character. Llewellyn and May took the stand in their own defense, testifying that their horses never could have caught the one ridden by Curly through the snowstorm, and that they had had little choice in how they had dispatched the outlaw. Without leaving the jury box, the panel of adjudicators returned a verdict of not guilty, thus ending the tragic saga of Lee "Curly" Grimes.

Helen Sieler

The Woman with Ten Lives

It was New Year's Eve 1936 when the sensational powder-house explosion rocked Sioux Falls. Fueled by three and one-half tons of black powder and thirty-three hundred pounds of dynamite, the force of the detonation was felt more than fifty miles away. The flash was visible for fifteen miles and the crater it created was twenty-five feet deep. The explosion shattered $20,000 in windowpanes in the immediate vicinity and several nearby farms were damaged.

And when the dust settled, there wasn't enough left of the man it was meant to kill to fill a baby-food jar.

The story of this Sioux Falls saga, unsurprisingly, did not start with a tale of innocence. Each of those involved was no stranger to crime and conspiracy. Each had a record and even the victim was a paroled convict.

In 1936 South Dakota and much of the Midwest was in the midst of its Dust Bowl days. Yellowish brown hazes alternated with black blizzards to blanket the Great Plains in misery. Children donned dust masks for school, homemakers did what they could to deal with the incessant filth and grime that permeated every part of their lives, and thousands of farmers simply watched as their crops dried up and blew away.

In South Dakota the lingering drought coupled with high winds and barren fields yielded skies that were darkened for days. In many places dust and dirt drifted like snow, killing what few cows remained and covering everything that didn't move. In the middle of the Great Depression, President Franklin Roosevelt would tell the American people, "I see one-third of the nation ill-housed, ill-clad, ill-nourished . . . [T]he test of our progress is not whether we add more to the abundance of those who have much; it is whether we provide enough for those who have too little." And by all accounts one downtrodden gang of heavies and hoodlums had finally decided they had far too little.

Three days before Christmas 1936, a gang and its moll conspired with a Sioux City, Iowa, jewelry-store owner to relieve him of some excess merchandise. He'd pocket a handsome insurance settlement and they'd each bag a grand in mad money. At least, that was the plan.

The gang consisted of a forty-five-year-old Sioux Falls bank robber and ex-convict named Lee Bradley; William Nesbeth, thirty-seven, a Sioux City bartender; Harry "Slim" Reeves, described as a thirty-six-year-old Sioux City desperado; Harold Baker, fifty-one; and his sweetheart, the pretty, dark-haired Helen Sieler, twenty-five, of Sioux City.

Sieler was no stranger to struggle or red-light districts, but she was out of her element. Three weeks before the crime she had left her husband, Edward Sieler, and taken up with the wild Harold Baker, a parolee who had spent time in a California prison. It was later learned that Baker's real name was Floyd H. Parker. Baker and Sieler were living on a quiet residential street in Omaha, Nebraska, under the names Mr. and Mrs. Roy Johnson. In late December the couple was visited by Bradley, Nesbeth, and Reeves, who were planning a robbery in Sioux City, just one hundred miles north of Omaha.

On the night of December 23, 1936, the four gangsters robbed the Ehlermann Wholesale Jewelry Company in Sioux City. When the group blew the safe on the second story of the Orpheum Building, the blast showered glass down on the crowd standing in line in front of the theater below. Reported stolen was $36,000 in miscellaneous jewelry and $1,000 in cash.

Police suspected an inside job from the beginning, particularly when they noted the acetylene tanks and torches conveniently stored in the jewelry firm's vault. A couple of weeks later, the *Daily Argus-Leader* in nearby Sioux Falls would report that "peculiar details of the crime are still under investigation."

Meanwhile, following the heist, the gangsters fled first to Omaha, then to Norfolk, Nebraska, and Yankton, South Dakota, before holing up in separate hotels in Sioux Falls. When their promised payoff didn't immediately materialize due to the ongoing police investigation of the robbery, they began to turn on each other. Baker and Mrs. Sieler talked of returning to Sioux City and turning themselves in. The suggestion was not met with enthusiasm by the couple's accomplices, who were afraid that Baker and Sieler would implicate them in the crime. To protect themselves, the other members of the gang began to conspire against Baker and Sieler.

On New Year's Eve, Bradley, Nesbeth, and Reeves suggested to Baker and Sieler that they steal some more dynamite—the key ingredient to their successful safecracking. The nearby powder house operated by the Larson Hardware Company had ample supplies, and so the group headed to the site five miles southeast of Sioux Falls shortly after sunset. Mrs. Sieler waited in the car while the men set about breaking into the depot.

Baker, dressed nattily in a tan camel-hair overcoat, black hat, deep tan shirt with figured brown necktie, a dark mixed suit, black oxfords, and grey socks, probably looked more a mobster than a burglar as he sauntered toward the powder house. As he reached the structure, Nesbeth hit Baker over the head with a hammer so hard it flew out of his hand. Baker fought back, but he was quickly subdued.

The three assailants then went after his girlfriend, dragging her into the dark depot. Nesbeth hit her on the head with his hammer. Another of her assailants kicked her in the face. Then the trio fired eight gunshots into her body and dragged her to a position next to the prone body of her boyfriend in the dynamite shack.

While Reeves ran back to start the getaway car, Nesbeth and Bradley fashioned a fuse long enough to give them ample time to get clear. Even they weren't sure what would happen when the cache of 300 twenty-five-pound cans of powder and thirty-three hundred pounds of dynamite went off. As the fuse burned and the gangsters fled eastward toward the Minnesota border, Mrs. Sieler regained consciousness and saw the inevitable fate that awaited her if she didn't move quickly. Dazed, with head wounds from the beating and eight bullets in her body, she crawled toward the doorway of the magazine and dragged herself out into the wintry night as far away as time would allow.

At 9:35 p.m., with the getaway car five to six miles away and Mrs. Sieler crawling through a snow-and-ice-filled ditch a couple of hundred yards from the powder house, the fuse completed its fateful mission.

The tremendous blast shook structures for miles around Sioux Falls, causing plaster walls to crack. Hundreds of windows in area businesses shattered from the concussion, which was heard and felt in Pipestone, Minnesota, over fifty miles away.

Police would later say that Mrs. Sieler had been hurled in the air two hundred feet by the explosion. The terrific detonation blew away the lower portions of the coat she was wearing and officers found two pieces of matching fabric three hundred feet away from where she landed. Already suffering from a beating and bullet wounds, she was taken to nearby Moe Hospital in serious condition and in severe shock.

When Mrs. Sieler awakened in her hospital room an hour after the blast, she first asked about her boyfriend and then started telling anyone who would listen about how her sad state of affairs had originated and who was responsible. By the next morning authorities had launched one of the most intense and far-flung manhunts in the region's history.

As police scoured the scene of the blast for any evidence of Baker, Sioux Falls salesman J. D. Higgins stopped by police headquarters to turn in a piece of flesh he had found about two hundred feet east of the powder house. Police believed it to be a remnant of Baker's shattered body and they turned it over to a physician for examination.

The next morning, Sieler told the *Daily Argus-Leader* that the trouble between Baker and his three killers began over a disagreement about the division of loot from the Sioux Falls robbery. Sieler said the band had burglarized a Nebraska store, stealing clothing, while she remained in the car. She also described in detail how Reeves, Nesbeth, and Bradley had assaulted her, shot her full of holes, and then left her to die beside her boyfriend in the dynamite shack.

"They first shot me once in the arm and then slugged me with a hammer," she told police. "They dragged me inside but I don't remember when they fired the other shots at me." That afternoon, doctors planned to "take x-ray pictures," the newspaper said. No slugs had been removed from her body and a bandage covered one eye where she was hit by a bullet. "It felt like my head was blown off when that one hit," she was quoted as saying.

After she gave police a full statement, the newspaper reported what would be the first of many surprises in the ensuing investigation of the powder-house blast. "It appeared unlikely she would face any charges. Police said she might be held as a material witness. She is under heavy guard of police and deputy sheriffs, fearful the gang might yet attempt to kill her."

As doctors began to treat Sieler's extensive injuries, they informed media outlets that she had been shot twice in the back, twice in the thigh, three times in the hip, and once in the face below an eye with a revolver of undetermined caliber.

When the dust and smoke had cleared the site of the explosion the next morning, officers measured a crater twenty-five feet wide, thirty-five feet long, and twenty-five feet deep. Scraps of iron and concrete had been hurled hundreds of yards in all directions. Warrants were issued and law enforcement agencies began issuing bulletins throughout South Dakota, Nebraska, and Iowa telling officers to be on the lookout for the three men they variously described as "a convicted bank robber, an underworld character, and a bartender." Regardless of their previous experience, they were all now sought on murder charges.

On January 2, 1937, as Sieler started her second day as the most notorious patient in Moe Hospital, her estranged husband walked

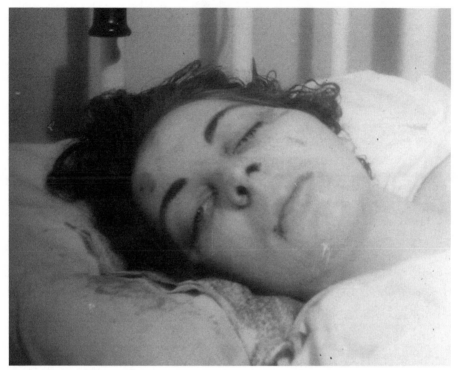

Helen Sieler hospitalized
Photo courtesy of Bill Patterson and the Minnehaha County (S. Dak.) Historical Society

through the door and into her room. Mr. Edward Sieler told a reporter that his wife had left him three weeks before this unfortunate series of events and that he had traveled all the way to Sioux Falls because he was still in love with her. Witnesses said Mrs. Sieler felt otherwise.

The seriousness of Sieler's injuries became more apparent when Dr. A. J. Moe gave her less than a fifty-fifty chance of survival. In addition to the injuries previously described, her doctor disclosed that her right leg had been frozen and was worsening, and that a bullet imbedded behind her right eye had caused the loss of sight in that eye.

While police continued their manhunt, health-department laboratory technician Harry Falconer examined what little remained of Harold Baker. Scouring the area of the blast, searchers had been disappointed to find only the bit of flesh, a bone fragment, and a small piece of cloth that appeared to be part of a man's trousers. Sieler had given police a detailed description of what Baker had been wearing when he was killed, right down to his pink silk underwear.

Murder warrants issued by Sioux Falls judge Lewis Larson named "Lee Bradley, alias Tom Tobin, South Dakota bank robber, and former convict; William Nesbeth, also know as Bill Nesbeth, Sioux City bartender; and Harry "Slim" Reeves, Sioux City underworld character."

As Mrs. Sieler struggled against death in the hospital three days after the explosion, Sioux Falls police chief Henry Morstad discounted a statement attributed to him that the powder-house blast "had been felt in San Francisco." He told the local newspaper that "he had not made any such comment, neither had he heard any reports that seismograph instruments on the west coast had recorded the blast."

When fugitive warrants were issued on January 4, federal agents joined the search for the three desperados who had crossed state lines after committing a felony. The same day, fearing reprisals from the gang, Chief Morstad doubled the guard around the hospital room of Mrs. Sieler after officers received reports that three men armed with pistols and a submachine gun were seen leaving Ottumwa, Iowa.

Finally, the search began to bear fruit. That night, Reeves was captured in a farmer's garage one and one-half miles south of Sioux City, after law officers received a tip from an undisclosed source as to the gangster's whereabouts. The capture was without confrontation, according to authorities. When Sheriff W. R. Tice and a deputy knocked on the door of the garage, Reeves reportedly asked, "Is that you, Bill?" When the sheriff responded in the affirmative, Reeves opened the garage door and was greeted by the wrong end of several weapons leveled at him. "All right, I won't give you any trouble," the man said in surrender.

Under intense grilling by law officers, Reeves admitted he had been with the gang that set off the powder-house blast on New Year's Eve, but he denied having taken part in the jewelry-store robbery or the murder of Baker and the attempted slaughter of his sweetheart. When informed that Reeves had claimed he tried to save Mrs. Sieler by pulling her away from the powder house, the hospitalized woman said Reeves was lying and that he "was the first to shoot me. I saw him shoot me and he knows it."

Reeves finally admitted to participating in the robbery and was sentenced to forty-three years in prison.

As weeks went by, Mrs. Sieler's condition gradually improved. Nearly two months passed before officers caught up to William Nesbeth, the thirty-seven-year-old Sioux City hoodlum. Unarmed, Nesbeth offered no resistance when he was arrested in a small hotel in downtown Oklahoma City where he had been staying for three weeks. He was returned to Sioux Falls to face charges of murdering Baker. Investigators reported that, under questioning, Nesbeth had admitted he played a part in the ordeal.

On trial in Sioux Falls three months later, Nesbeth took the stand and denied having played any part in the dynamite blast slaying of Baker or the attempted murder of Helen Sieler. His claims came after his former partner, Reeves, had testified that it was Nesbeth who had hit both Baker and Sieler with a hammer. Every time prosecutors referred to the small glass jar that held the remains of Baker, Helen Sieler wept uncontrollably.

As his wife and mother watched him testify, Nesbeth put the blame for the murder on Reeves and the still-uncaptured Bradley. But the jury didn't buy his story and, after just ninety minutes of deliberation, convicted Nesbeth of murder. The conviction carried a mandatory life sentence.

As Nesbeth was led away to begin his long term behind bars, E. D. Barron, the state's attorney, told reporters that Sieler, who had been held in the county jail as a material witness since being discharged from the hospital, would be released and allowed to go home to live with her mother in Sioux City. The twenty-six-year-old woman still carried eight bullets in her body from the ordeal, he noted.

Two months after the judge sentenced Nesbeth to life in prison, the last fugitive in the crime was caught while working in a hay field near

Yakima, Washington. The arrest of Lee Bradley, forty-five, was triggered by a tip from an unidentified reader of detective-story magazines, police said. Extradited to South Dakota to stand trial, Bradley pleaded guilty to first-degree murder charges and was sentenced to life in prison, his third prison term in twenty years of crime.

Handcuffed to the local sheriff, Bradley replied to every question the judge asked with a mix of candor and humor. "No, I'm not proud of my record," he told Judge John T. Medin. "Money gained through crime comes much harder than when it is honestly earned." He told the judge that he had never been in trouble as a young man, when his father's guidance precluded consideration of crime.

In his conversation with the judge before sentencing, Bradley admitted that he had lit the fuse at the powder house while in a daze from consuming alcohol and marijuana. When the judge suggested that they had traveled to the site with the express purpose of murdering Baker and Sieler, Bradley objected. "We did not," he replied emphatically. "You know marijuana and liquor combined can create an awful mess. It just happened on the spur of the moment." Following the lengthy discussion, Judge Medin sentenced Bradley to the South Dakota penitentiary for the rest of Bradley's natural life.

With the last of the three murderers caught, tried, and sentenced to long terms, it might have ended the news coverage of the trio and the dynamite blast that had ushered in 1937 for Sioux Falls. However, seven years after Bradley began his prison term, Nesbeth walked away from the state penitentiary while serving as a trustee, just three years before he was eligible for parole. He remained free for three and one-half years, before two grade school boys found him living in a cave near St. Paul and alerted police. Recaptured, Nesbeth was return to prison and served four more years before being released in May 1954.

Helen Sieler, who had survived being beaten and shot eight times, who had escaped all criminal charges, and who was once branded by a newspaper as "the woman with ten lives," was never heard from again.

Stella and Bennie Dickson
South Dakota's Own Bonnie and Clyde

For her sixteenth birthday Stella Dickson robbed a bank. For her seventeenth birthday she was sent to a federal prison.

Little Stella Redenbaugh fell for the older, tousle-headed Bennie Dickson during the worst of the Great Depression. He was a promising boxer and former Boy Scout who one day hoped to be a lawyer. In 1918 he and his brother, Spencer, had even rescued a woman when she attempted to drown herself in a local pond. The heroic act led the Kansas governor to propose the boys, who lived in Kansas at the time, for the Carnegie Medal. But somewhere along his life's journey, those who knew him said Bennie had proceeded down a wayward path.

When Bennie married Stella, Stella wasn't yet sixteen. Money was scarce, jobs were nonexistent, and very few in the Midwest had an easy go of it. Undeterred by conventional wisdom, the starry-eyed couple vacationed at a family cabin on Lake Preston in eastern South Dakota. As Stella's special birthday approached, they apparently didn't think much about cake and candles. They thought about cash.

At about 2:30 p.m. on August 25, 1938—just a half hour before the Elkton Corn Exchange Bank's scheduled summer closing—Bennie marched into the foyer and saw the bank's two employees on duty, cashier R. F. Petschow and bookkeeper Elaine Lovley, engaged at the main business counter. Bennie approached, leveled his revolver at the pair, and calmly said, "This is a holdup. Do exactly as I say and there will be no trouble and nobody hurt."

Should a patron enter the bank, Bennie instructed Petschow to lead him or her to the floor behind the counter. When informed by the cashier that the delayed time lock to the bank's vault would not open until 3:00 p.m., the composed criminal said he'd wait, which he did— for thirty-five minutes.

During the period no less than twenty individuals entered the bank, including the institution's president, L. C. Foreman. All were scrutinized and quietly led to their holding place on the floor behind the teller's counter. As each customer entered the bank, "the bandit had them hand over their currency, but with an apparent desire not to take money from private individuals, except in instances where indications were that the loss could be well afforded, [and] he had Mr. Petschow look up the balances of each individual customer, to whom in most instances he casually returned their money," the *Elkton Record* reported a week later.

"Mrs. Koehn in the excitement incident to the proceedings dropped a $20 bill for which she had come in to get change, and the robber in a gentlemanly manner picked it up and handed it back to her," the newspaper added. "Roy Kramer had $240 in currency, and after ascertaining that this was his private money and not the property of the Standard Oil Co., and the records showing only a small credit balance, this currency was returned to him."

When Bennie had acquired sufficient resources with which to secure a birthday present for his newlywed wife as well as finance his imminent departure, he herded the bank officials and their customers into the vault, closed the heavy door, and made his getaway. A short time later, the bankers flipped an emergency switch within the vault intended for just such a purpose. The switch activated a warning light in Elkton's Dressel Store, and the captives were soon released.

Within minutes, bank officials telephoned news of the brazen daylight robbery to Sioux Falls, and within two hours of the holdup, investigators with the state and federal departments of justice were on the scene. Bennie had been wearing gloves, so efforts to find his fingerprints proved futile. But officials were aware that Bennie had an accomplice, even though they didn't have a clue who either of them was or where they had gone.

With the help of Sheriff Hank Claussen, law enforcement authorities spent the next few days securing evidence they hoped would lead to the apprehension of the desperados. The *Elkton Record* pronounced, "One fact which may be of value in tracing the pair by checking the circulation of the stolen money is that a shipment of new currency had been received on the day of the holdup, and the serial numbers of these bills will be a matter of record."

A week after the crime, Bennie and Stella were leading a life on the lam with as much as $2,500 in cash. But after lying low for two months, their financial reserves began to dwindle. It was time to hit another bank. On the eve of Halloween, they arrived in Brookings, a modest college town in extreme eastern South Dakota that was just recovering from its annual hell-raising Hobo Day. Bennie and Stella would bring life back to the party.

When officials of Northwestern Security National Bank opened the doors for business at 8:30 a.m. on Monday, October 31, they were greeted by a handsome young couple equipped with a machine gun and a sawed-off shotgun. The dynamic duo calmly waited for the delayed time lock to open at 11:00 a.m.

The previous Saturday's celebration of Hobo Day had ensured a brisk Monday morning business at the bank, the *Elkton Record* reported three days after the robbery, in a story adjacent to the newspaper's near-breathless announcement that *Boys Town* starring Spencer Tracy would soon come to the Elks Theatre. When Bennie and Stella arrived in Brookings, a tree-lined bastion of academia, they may have sensed easy pickings. In the two and one-half hours that the heavily armed pair stood vigil, more than one hundred people walked in and out of the bank, making their weekend deposits and loan payments, getting change, and conducting other transactions. None of them was ever aware that they stood one misstep from two desperate fugitives in the midst of pulling off a most daring raid.

At 11:00 a.m. the time lock opened, allowing access to the vault. Bennie and Stella quickly stuffed as much of the available cash as they could into bank bags and chose Northwestern Security officials R. M. DePuy and Jon Torsey as hostages. Coolly, the four left the institution unnoticed and began their getaway. Bennie and Stella got in the front seat of their black Buick while DePuy and Torsey were instructed to stand on the running boards on the outside of the vehicle. Then the car bolted forward. A few blocks later, when it appeared they had not been pursued, "Bennie slowed the sedan and his petite blond-haired accomplice dismissed the bankers with a smile and a good-bye."

A short time later, authorities received reports of the vehicle traveling at a high rate of speed southwest of Elkton. Officials quickly responded but were unable to apprehend the pair.

As they sped down gravel back roads in a cloud of dust, the Depression-era outlaws must have thought themselves another Bonnie and Clyde. Just four years earlier, Bonnie Parker and Clyde Barrow had terrorized the Midwest with a series of bold bank heists and epic gun battles with authorities. After four years of outrunning law officers and capturing the imagination of an entire nation, Bonnie and Clyde died on May 23, 1934, in a hail of gunfire near their Bienville Parish, Louisiana, hideout, struck down by a posse of heavily armed Texas and Louisiana lawmen.

As immortal as only youth can imagine themselves to be, Bennie and Stella didn't likely dwell on Bonnie and Clyde's tragic fate. In their black Buick the newlyweds carried $47,233 in cash and bonds from the Halloween holdup at the Brookings bank, and they were intent on putting as much ground between themselves and pursuing posses as they could.

But the police had all the time in the world. When they eventually tracked Bennie and Stella to a tourist campground in Topeka, Kansas, on November 24, authorities closed in on the pair. After a brief gunfight Bennie and Stella separated, both making good their escape. Bennie fled in his Buick to South Clinton, Iowa, stole another vehicle, then doubled back to Topeka to retrieve his bride at a prearranged rendezvous point one day after the shootout.

As the couple traveled to Michigan, authorities made several attempts to capture the fugitives. In one incident, while being pursued by a patrol car, Stella grabbed a gun and shot out the cruiser's tires, earning her the nickname, "Sure Shot" Stella. During the shootout a cop's bullet grazed Stella's forehead, leaving a scar she would carry for a lifetime. In a series of confrontations, the bank robbers took three men hostage, stole getaway cars in Michigan and Indiana, and eluded lawmen on country back roads.

Now far from home and aggressively pursued by lawmen from several states, the young couple reached St. Louis and tried to blend in. When Bennie was lured to a hamburger stand by a female informant on April 6, 1939, he discovered too late that the FBI was closing in. As he attempted to flee, a young federal agent put at least four holes in Bennie's back, creating a sixteen-year-old widow and putting an end to Bennie's short lifetime of regrets.

Apparently alerted to her husband's death, Stella fled 250 miles west to Kansas City. When authorities caught up with her the next day, she was unarmed, carried $70, and was wearing three rings, including the wedding set with seven diamonds that Bennie had provided. With the fight knocked out of her and the romance gone, little Stella Dickson was apprehended without any resistance. When arrested, she also possessed a key to a New Orleans apartment and a poem Bennie had penned. It read, "In the eyes of men I am not just/But in your eyes, O life, I see justification/You have taught me that my path is right if I am true to you."

Returned to South Dakota for trial on bank robbery charges in federal district court in Deadwood, Stella reportedly listened to the proceedings while clutching a doll in her arms. Whether she did so to emphasize her youth to the jury or merely because the doll gave her comfort was never determined. The *Mitchell Daily Republic* claimed she looked "more like a schoolgirl than a gun moll awaiting the proceedings of the court on charges of bank robbery including the taking of hostages, a possible capital offense."

But Judge Lee A. Wyman did determine that Stella was guilty of taking other people's money at gunpoint. Citing her youth and the corrupting influence of her older, now-dead husband, the judge sentenced Stella to two ten-year sentences to be served concurrently. On the day she walked into the West Virginia federal prison for women, she turned seventeen.

While the shock of confinement and the loss of Bennie must have case-hardened her heart, Stella spent her time in prison taking vocational technical courses and thinking about freedom. When she was paroled in 1946, she was just twenty-four years old.

Following her release, she served a stint as a flight attendant, fixed her own plumbing and built her own fence, cared for her disabled brother, and had a lengthy career as a clerk at Kmart. She remarried twice over the course of years, but later in life admitted to a Kansas City neighbor that she had only ever truly loved one man.

As she aged, Stella became increasingly reclusive, adopting more than a half dozen pets from the animal shelter at which she volunteered. She led a quiet life with few friends save the furry ones she rescued from a hell she had personally known. Her austere lifestyle eventually earned her a pardon for her youthful crimes from President Nixon, but few who knew her in the last decades of her life remotely suspected that little Stella had ever been in trouble with the law.

When she died on September 10, 1995, following an extended illness, no obituary marked the passing of "Sure Shot" Stella, one of the youngest and prettiest outlaws to ever plague the plains.

George Sitts

Lone Man Electrocuted

On a cold winter night in January 1946, convicted murderer George Sitts was racing across western South Dakota in a stolen car, well armed and hell-bent on avoiding the authorities who were conducting a nationwide manhunt for the escaped convict.

When he was pulled over for speeding through an intersection near Spearfish, Sitts calmly stopped his car, opened his door, stepped from the sedan, pulled out his pistol, and gunned down two veteran South Dakota lawmen. As the officers lay bleeding on the pavement, Sitts methodically fired bullets into each of their heads, rifled the bodies for money and guns, and went on his merry way.

A Minnesota native, Sitts would be the only man ever put to death by electrocution in the state of South Dakota. And he went to his death telling executioners that they were the only ones who had ever helped him escape from jail.

Born in 1914 in the small farming community of LeRoy, Minnesota, located on the Iowa border, fifty miles south of Rochester, Sitts was regarded among his grade school peers as likely to achieve success. Later, he would be remembered in his hometown as a quiet, studious, well-mannered young boy who would hurry home from school to do chores for his ailing grandmother.

Then as now, the town of LeRoy was surrounded by farms, its prosperity linked to the region's fertile soils and the Chicago Great Western Railroad, which ran through town. According to the 1910 U.S. Census, only 724 people lived in the entire township. The decidedly rural lifestyle led young Sitts to become an avid reader. He favored lurid fiction and stories of frontier exploits and criminal deeds. He also loved guns and worked to become a crack shot.

Sitts's boyhood ambition was to become a great boxer and he probably huddled, as did millions of Americans, close to the radio in his house to listen as Jack Dempsey defended his heavyweight title several times in the 1920s. Sitts would eventually box under the name "Kid Kramer" in bouts at St. Paul, Sioux City, San Francisco, and other places. His broken and flattened nose would attest to the level of his ability for the rest of his life.

His first of many encounters with the law occurred when Sitts was just nineteen. Convicted of carrying concealed weapons and receiving stolen property, he spent ninety days in an Iowa jail. Three years later, Sitts was given a ten-year sentence in Minnesota for burglary. He was paroled in 1941, but was returned to prison the next year for violating parole. There he would sit for three years before being released again in 1944, at age thirty. In the midst of World War II, jobs were plentiful in the Pacific Northwest and Sitts set out for Portland, Oregon. He married at some point, but later told a reporter that he'd separated from his wife shortly after their nuptials.

According to scant records of his life and movements, in late 1945 Sitts traveled back to Minneapolis to see a girlfriend. On arriving in the Twin Cities, he learned that she had moved to Texas. Unemployed and broke, but still wanting to follow her to the Lone Star State, Sitts tried to get some easy cash by robbing a Minneapolis liquor store on December 12, 1945. When things went wrong, Sitts killed the store's clerk, Erik Johansson, and fled the scene.

Law officers trapped Sitts just sixty miles away and arrested him for killing Johansson. With a criminal record that was quickly catching up to him, Sitts made it easy on prosecutors and pleaded guilty to second-degree murder. He was given a life sentence and held in the Hennepin County Jail while awaiting transfer to the Stillwater State Prison. But he didn't remain idle.

Working with three fellow inmates, Sitts acquired a hacksaw blade and spent the next three weeks sawing through two bars of his cell. Finishing the project the day before his scheduled transfer to prison, Sitts was joined by two auto thieves and a forger when he slugged a radio dispatcher and broke out of jail.

Two days after the breakout, on the lam and now facing escape charges in addition to his life sentence, Sitts stole a car and headed west. One of his fellow escapees, nineteen-year-old Robert Morris, was quickly recaptured, but Sitts remained at large. Police were kept busy following up reports in Madelia, a small town southwest of the Twin Cities, where they investigated a sighting of Sitts. In Sioux Falls the reported theft of another vehicle was also tied to Sitts. Law enforcement agencies throughout the nation were notified of the escape and given descriptions of the convicts and the stolen vehicle. Roadblocks were set up, but they were unsuccessful.

In the preinterstate 1940s South Dakota was a web of interlaced state and county highways and dusty gravel roads that followed each section line to the horizon and beyond. Keeping tabs on all of them was a virtual impossibility. Authorities could only respond to sightings and reports of gas and car thefts and man roadblocks at strategic points.

Sticking to the back roads as he headed west through South Dakota in a stolen car five days after the jailbreak, Sitts was forced to get gasoline were he could find it. At least one newspaper reported that a gun had been stolen from a Newell-area rancher. If Sitts was the perpetrator, he need only have taken the highway twenty-five miles from the sheep ranching town of Newell west to Belle Fourche, then south another thirteen miles to the junction with Highway 10, where fate dealt him his final hand.

On the night of January 24, 1946, Special Agent Tom Matthews of the State Bureau of Investigation and Sheriff Dave Malcolm of Butte County were manning a roadblock on the north edge of Spearfish. A college town tucked on the north range of the Black Hills and home to one of the oldest fish hatcheries in the West, Spearfish was normally tranquil and quiet. Sitts's escape had changed all that.

Agent Matthews was the forty-eight-year-old son of local ranchers and had attended Black Hills Teachers College. At eighteen he was racing cars, and by the time he was twenty, he had his own herd of cattle on his father's well-known T-7 Cattle & Horse Ranch south of Gillette. He also had a wife and a six-year-old son.

Sheriff Malcolm had been born in Scotland and came to the United States as a six-year-old boy. In 1895 his family settled in Hot Springs before moving north to a homestead near Nisland. He married a Spearfish gal and tried turns at farming and mining before serving two terms as deputy sheriff of Butte County. Well liked and involved, Malcolm ran for sheriff, won, and took office in January 1945. On this night a year later, his wife, Edith, was probably at their Spearfish home caring for Elizabeth Ann, their eight-month-old daughter.

Just a few miles west from Matthews and Malcolm loomed the vast expanses of Wyoming and Montana. They were on the lookout for a 1940 green Ford coach carrying an armed man, six foot three, with dark hair and a week-old beard.

Eventually justice found their man, but justice did not prevail, as two law officers were dead, gunned down near their police vehicles. Sitts would later tell the Associated Press that Agent Matthews had pulled his car over as it whipped through the intersection of Highways 14 and 85. Matthews directed Sitts to return to the intersection where Sheriff Malcolm waited, and Sitts complied. As the two cars rolled up to Malcolm's police cruiser, a truck approached and Malcolm backed his vehicle out of the way. Sitts said he stepped from his car and shot Matthews, who fell to the pavement. Seconds later he shot Malcolm. Because "they were still moving," Sitts fired one more shot into each man's head. He then searched the bodies, taking some money, and (always the gun-lover) Matthews's Luger pistol.

Following the discovery of the bodies, law enforcement set up an immediate dragnet. State and county officers were joined in the search by agents from the FBI and the hunt eventually extended nationwide. Police scoured the Black Hills for a week and more residents than usual began carrying firearms. Authorities located the sedan that Sitts had abandoned on a detour about ten miles south of the scene of the slayings. But when no trace of Sitts was found after a week, authorities appealed to the pubic for assistance in offering any nugget of information that would lead to the cop killer's arrest.

The *Rapid City Journal* published a photo of a dark-haired, thin-faced Sitts. In a story posted by the AP on January 31, Les Price, chief agent of the state attorney general's law enforcement division, said the search had "turned from following hot leads to routine investigation." He urged the public to report "any bits of information" and warned them not to leave keys in the ignition of their vehicles. "It's everybody's job to help find this killer," Price said. "We know who we're after, but the scene of operations is so vast, we must have help from the general public."

Meanwhile, tired, cold, and miserable, thirty-two-year-old George Sitts was searching for a way out. After shooting the officers and getting his car stuck as he drove toward Deadwood, he had abandoned the vehicle and wandered a mile before finding an old stone schoolhouse far from any town. He hid out in the attic even as a posse searched the main floor.

Suffering from the cold, he managed to burn his shoes while starting a fire to keep warm. With no food and frozen feet, Sitts decided to move on. He set out for Deadwood with his feet wrapped in burlap. When he reached the town, cold and tired, he entered the first house he could find and hid out in the basement. For seven days he lived in the cellar of the house while its owner, former Deadwood police chief Ross Dunn, was scouring the hills looking for Sitts. When Mrs. Dunn left a basement door open a week after he arrived, Sitts borrowed a pair of the owner's shoes and fled.

On a cold Sunday morning in February, Sitts suddenly appeared in the backseat of local filling station operator Leonard Ronneberg's car and ordered him to drive to Wyoming. After making Ronneberg buy gas for the car in Beulah, Wyoming, Sitts handed him $10 and told him to get out. Alerted to the carjacking, Wyoming sent nearly three dozen patrol cars in pursuit of Sitts. Listening to radio news reports, driving hard and fast on the snowy back roads past the ranching towns of Buffalo and Casper, Sitts got stuck twice and at gunpoint forced locals to assist him. When he was stuck a third time 370 miles from Deadwood, two county sheriff's deputies approached him asking, "Need any help?" They then promptly arrested him without a struggle. Sitts would say later that, had he known they were lawmen, he would have shot it out.

Sitts had terrorized western South Dakota for eleven days after gunning down Matthews and Malcolm. Following his arrest, as county boards, Black Hills groups, and even the *Rapid City Journal* handed out rewards, Sitts was returned to South Dakota. Within a month he was on trial for the murder of Agent Matthews. Assigned to defend him was Deadwood attorney Jon T. Heffron. Heading the prosecution was Attorney General George T. Mickelson, later elected governor, and he presented a strong case. Heffron offered no testimony for Sitts, other than arguing for a mistrial on the grounds that the jury was biased and that Sitts should actually be on trial for manslaughter because he had acted "in the heat of passion—not in malice" when he gunned down the two officers.

It took the jury two hours and seventeen minutes to find Sitts guilty of murdering Matthews. They recommended execution. Nine days later, Circuit Judge Charles Hayes ordered Sitts put to death. The condemned man showed no emotion as the sentence was pronounced. The state elected not to try Sitts for the murder of Malcolm.

In an age when repeated death sentence appeals commonly last well over a decade, Sitts's stay in prison would be relatively short—just one year and eight days. The brief stay was apparently to his satisfaction. In an exchange of correspondence with a Louisiana prisoner, Sitts wrote his criminal friend, "I'd prefer to die rather than spend a lifetime in prison."

As his death day approached, Sitts talked more to his jailers and reportedly found the Bible. Two days before his scheduled execution, New York's *Sunday News* led the front page with the headline, "CALCU-LATING KILLER" WILL TRY OUT CHAIR. Sitts's final requests were few: just a cake of soap and a clean shirt. For his final meal he ate chow mien, tea, bread and butter, and ice cream. The warden even threw in a piece of cake. Witnesses to the impending death waited in a wet snowfall outside the prison's double steel doors.

Even though South Dakota had introduced the electric chair as the manner of execution in 1939, it hadn't been used in eight years. Three men previously sentenced to die in it had had their sentences commuted to life in prison. Sitts would be the first.

Shortly after midnight on April 8, 1947, after having had his head shaved and been led to the electric chair, three straps were secured around Sitts's chest and arms. An electrode containing a wet sponge was placed inside a $3.55 football helmet, purchased the previous day, which was then placed on his head. Asked if he had any final words, Sitts offered a wry joke to his executioners and the witnesses assembled for his death. "In all my experience, this is the first time the authorities helped me escape prison," he said, right before twenty-three hundred volts of electricity surged through his body. It was 12:15 a.m.

The gallery was quiet as Sitts was pronounced dead a few minutes later, his body destined for an unmarked grave in a county cemetery. Forty-two invited witnesses watched Sitts die. Most were law officers, prison guards, and state officials, as well as six newspapermen and three doctors.

Floyd Short, a state investigator who had been friends with officers Matthews and Malcolm and had transported Sitts to justice after his capture in Wyoming, had volunteered to throw the switch carrying electricity to Sitts. Ironically, Short had been charged with murder for the fatal shooting of a Harding County ranch hand who busted out of jail in 1930, after being arrested for rustling sheep. Short, however, had been acquitted.

Following the execution, Short was quoted as saying, "When Sitts began to twitch, I began to smile."

Bibliography

Chief Two Sticks

Brown, Dee. *Bury My Heart at Wounded Knee: An Indian History of the American West*. New York: Henry Holt and Company, 1970.

Carr, G. Sam. "Sioux Chief Two Sticks." *Wild West* (June 2001).

Newson, T. M. *Thrilling Scenes among the Indians. With a Graphic Description of Custer's Last Fight with Sitting Bull*. Chicago and New York: Belford, Clarke and Company, 1884. http://digital.library.wisc .edu/1711.dl/History.

Reno, Marcus A. *The Official Record of a Court of Inquiry Convened at Chicago, Illinois, January 13, 1879, by the President of the United States upon the Request of Major Marcus A. Reno, 7th U.S. Cavalry, to Investigate His Conduct at the Battle of the Little Big Horn, June 25–26, 1876*. Pacific Palisades, Calif.: U. S. Government, 1951. http://digital .library.wisc.edu/1711.dl/History.Reno.

Utley, Robert M. *The Lance and the Shield: The Life and Times of Sitting Bull*. New York: Henry Holt and Company, 1993.

Madame Vestal

Carr, G. Sam. "Boone May Brought Outlaws to Justice." *Deadwood Magazine* (January/February 1998).

Deadwood Daily Pioneer. "Story of a Life of a Deadwood Romance," April 11, 1924.

Flakus, Greg. "Gunfighters and Lawmen." *Wild West* (December 1998).

Floyd, Dustin D. "Outlaws." *Deadwood Magazine* (December 2006).

Kelly, Bill. "Lady Gamblers of the Wild West: The Amazing Madame Vestal." St. Louis, Mo.: The GameMaster Online, 1999.

Lame Johnny

Carr, G. Sam. "Nemesis of Outlaws." *Deadwood Magazine* (January/February 1998).

Halstead, Orval. *Our Yesterdays.* Custer, S.Dak.: Eastern Custer County Historical Society, date unknown.

Hasselstrom, Linda M. *Roadside History of South Dakota.* Missoula, Mont.: Mountain Press Publishing Company, 1994.

Klock, Irma. "Boone May Heavy-Handed Station Agent in Black Hills." *Rapid City Journal,* November 30, 1997.

Lawton, R. T. "Necktie Party Ended Lame Outlaw's Career." *Deadwood Magazine* (Fall 2002).

Patterson, Richard. *Historical Atlas of the Outlaw West.* Boulder, Colo.: Johnson Publishing Company, 1985.

James Leighton Gilmore

Black Hills Daily Times (Deadwood, South Dakota), August 13, 1881; December 20, 1882.

Dakota Territory Supreme Court Rulings, May 1882 Term; United States v. James Leighton, alias, etc. Yankton, Dakota Territory, July 1882.

Johannsen, Albert. *The House of Beadle and Adams and Its Dime and Nickel Novels*. Norman: University of Oklahoma Press, 1950.

Ohio Press, October 21, 1882; March 10, 1890.

Steubenville Weekly Gazette, October 21, November 24, December 22, 1882.

Bud Stevens

Corson County News, September 14, 1939.

Griffith, Rose. "The Trading Post of LeBeau." *True West Magazine* (date unknown).

Mobridge Tribune, December 18, 1909; March 25, April 1, 1910; May 28, 1981; April 30, 2003.

Philip Weekly Review, December 16, 1909.

Potter County News, December 16, 1909.

South Dakota Historical Collections (vol. 30). Pierre: South Dakota State Historical Society, 2007.

Walworth County Record, December 18, 25, 1909; January 1, March 26, 1910.

Ziebach County Historical Society. *South Dakota's Ziebach County: History of the Prairie*. Dupree, S.Dak.: Author, 1982.

Charles Brown

Black Hills Daily Times, February 6, 1886; June 17, 1897.

Crisler, Frank. "Killer Halves Woman's Head with Meat Cleaver, Hanged Two Months Later." *Arlington Sun*, August 24, 2006.

Dakota Republican, July 22, 1897.

Deadwood Weekly Pioneer, May 20, 1897.

Watertown Public Opinion, July 23, 1897.

Wild Bill Hickok

Cheyenne Daily Leader, August 26, 1876.

Patterson, Richard. *Historical Atlas of the Outlaw West.* Boulder, Colo.: Johnson Publishing Company, 1985.

Rosa, Joseph G. *Wild Bill Hickok: The Man & His Myth.* Lawrence: University Press of Kansas, 1996.

Turner, Thadd M. *Wild Bill Hickok: Deadwood City—End of the Trail.* Boca Raton, Fla.: Old West Alive! Publishing, 2001.

Young, Richard Alan, and Judy Dockrey Young. *Outlaw Tales: Legends, Myths, and Folklore from America's Middle Border.* Little Rock, Ark.: August House Publishers, 1992.

Thomas Egan

Daily Argus-Leader, October 25, 1902.

Egan, C. John Jr. *Drop Him Till He Dies.* Sioux Falls, S.Dak.: Ex Machina Publishing Company, 1994.

Rapid City Journal, August 28, 2006.

Sioux Falls Times, December 6, 1881.

Union County Courier, December 14, 1881.

Crow Dog

Black Hills Daily Times, August 12, 20, 1881; March 16, 17, 18, 21, 24, 25, 30, 1882; April 26, 1882; July 8, 1882; October 25, 1882; November 15, 1882; December 20, 1882; January 8, 15, 1884; December 19, 1890.

Haney Lopez, Ian. *White by Law: The Legal Construction of Race.* New York and London: New York University Press, 2006.

Lee "Curly" Grimes

Black Hills Daily Times, February 4, 5, 7, 8, 11, 12, 13, 15, 17, 1880; August 25, 1880.

Carr, G. Sam. "Boone May Brought Outlaws to Justice." *Deadwood Magazine* (January/February 1998).

Engebretson, Doug. *Empty Saddles, Forgotten Names.* Aberdeen, S.Dak.: North Plains Press, 1982.

Klock, Irma May. "Boone May Heavy-Handed Station Agent in Early Hills." *Rapid City Journal,* November 30, 1997.

Spring, Agnes W. *The Cheyenne and Black Hills Stage and Express Routes.* Lincoln: Bison Book/University of Nebraska Press, 1948.

Helen Sieler

Daily Argus-Leader, January 1, 2, 3, 4, 5, 1937; February 27, 28, 1937; May 20, 22, 27, 1937; July 28, 1938; January 13, 1939; September 6, 1946; March 20, 24, 27, 1954.

Stella and Bennie Dickson

Cecil, Charles F. *Remember the Time.* Brookings, S.Dak.: Charles Cecil Publishing, 2002.

Elkton Record, September 1, November 3, 1938.

Interview. Dr. Matthew Cecil, professor of journalism, South Dakota State University, Brookings, South Dakota, April 2007.

Newton, Michael. *Encyclopedia of Robbers, Heists, and Capers.* New York: Facts on File, 2002.

George Sitts

Associated Press. "Chair Closes Criminal Career." *Daily Argus-Leader* (Sioux Falls, S.Dak.), April 8, 1947.

Associated Press. "Testimony Completed in Sitts Murder Trial." *Daily Argus-Leader* (Sioux Falls, S.Dak.), March 20, 1946.

Daily Argus-Leader, April 8, 1947.

New York Sunday News. "'Calculating Killer' Will Try Out Chair," April 6, 1947.

Rapid City Daily Journal, January 25, 31, 1946; February 24, April 8, 1947.

United Press International. "Prisoner Faces Murder Charge." *Daily Argus-Leader* (Sioux Falls, S.Dak.), February 7, 1946.

About the Author

A fourth-generation South Dakotan, Tom Griffith attended the University of London before he was graduated from the University of Wisconsin-Eau Claire. He worked as a reporter, photographer, and managing editor of award-winning newspapers in Arizona, Montana, and South Dakota before serving as director of communications for the Mount Rushmore Preservation Fund, a nationwide campaign that raised $25 million to preserve and improve the mountain memorial.

In addition to writing articles for dozens of newspapers and magazines, Griffith is the author of five books, including *America's Shrine of Democracy*, with a foreword by President Ronald Reagan; *South Dakota*, a comprehensive guide to the state distributed worldwide; and *Greeno: A Winning Tradition*, with a foreword by NBC's Tom Brokaw. Griffith's travel writing, news articles, and features have appeared in newspapers and magazines from New York to New Zealand, including the *Rapid City Journal*, *Wisconsin State Journal*, *Billings Gazette*, *Bismarck Tribune*, *St. Paul Pioneer Press*, and *New Zealand Herald*, as well as a host of periodicals including *Historic Traveler*, *Midwest Living*, *AAA Home & Away*, *AAA Living*, *Native Peoples*, *Country Inns*, *Hadassah*, *SkyWest*, and *Western Horseman*.

Griffith is an active member of the Society of American Travel Writers and Western Writers of America. As a contributing writer to major publishing companies for nearly two decades, including The Globe Pequot Press, Griffith also has coauthored more than three dozen volumes, including *Fodor's USA*, *Healthy Escapes*, *Great American Vacations*, *The Old West*, *The Lewis & Clark Trail*, *South Dakota's Black Hills & Badlands*, and *National Parks of the West*. His travel writing has taken him to forty-five countries. Griffith and his wife, Nyla, make their home in the Black Hills of South Dakota. In their spare time they enjoy trout fishing, motorcycling, and traveling.